insight text guide

Roie Thomas

Cloudstreet

Tim Winton

insight

▸ innovative ▸ engaging ▸ evolving

First published in 2009. Reprinted 2012, 2014, 2018, 2020.

Insight Publications Pty Ltd
3/350 Charman Road
Cheltenham VIC 3192
Australia
Tel: +61 3 8571 4950
Fax: +61 3 8571 0257
Email: books@insightpublications.com.au

www.insightpublications.com.au

National Library of Australia Cataloguing-in-Publication entry:
Thomas, Roie.
Tim Winton's Cloudstreet : insight text guide / Roie Thomas.
1st ed.
9781921411014 (pbk.)
Insight text guide.
Bibliography.
For secondary school age.
Winton, Tim, 1960- . Cloudstreet.
A823.3

Other ISBNs:
9781925175066 (digital)
9781925175394 (bundle: print + digital)

Printed in Australia by Ligare.

contents

CHARACTER MAP

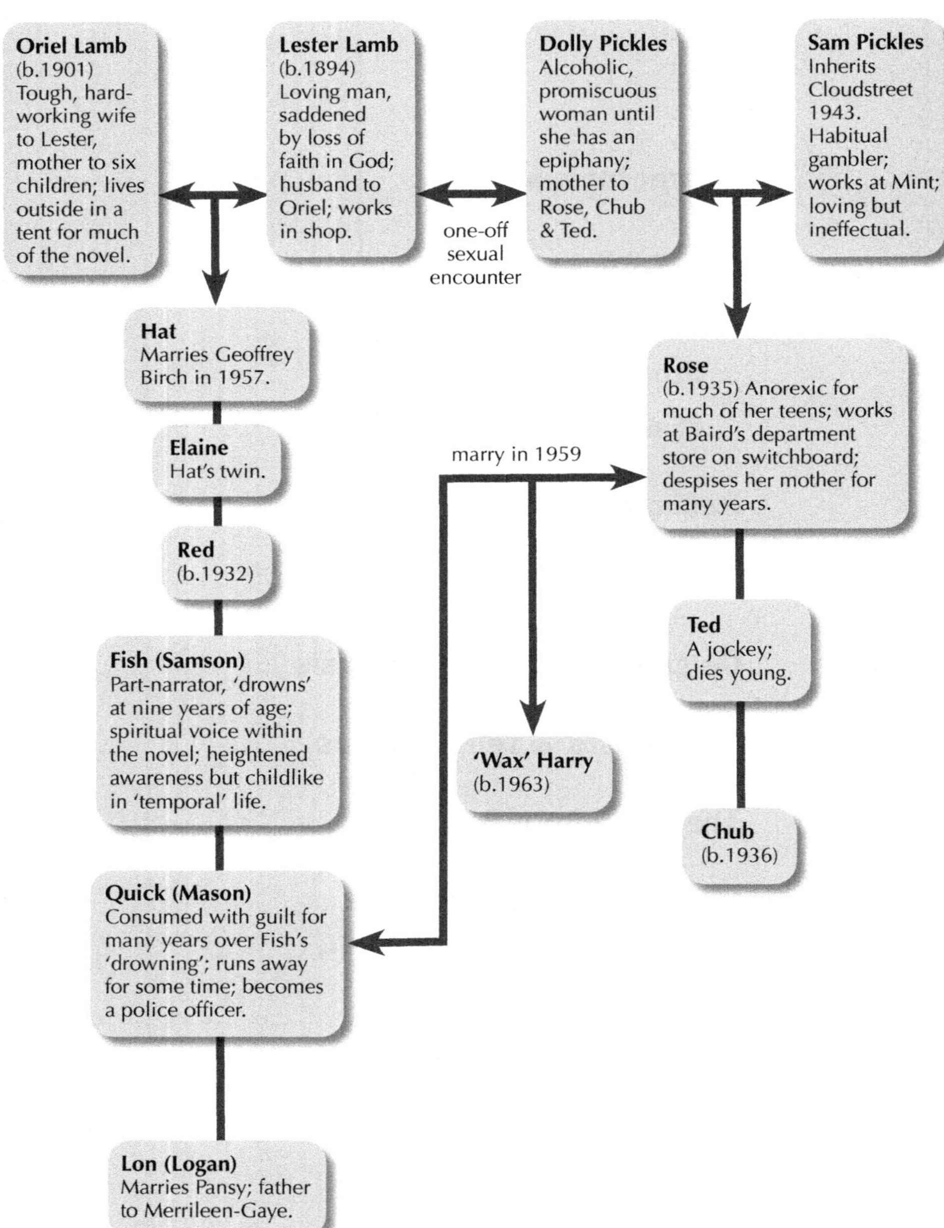

OVERVIEW

About the author

Tim Winton is West Australian through and through, having lived there most of his life with the exception of brief periods in Paris, Greece and Ireland. His life has almost always been in coastal towns, and his love of the sea is often reflected in his writing. Born in 1960, Winton began writing at an early age, and he has commented that it was fortunate he was successful as a writer, as he had no other career ideas. He graduated in Creative Writing from the Western Australian Institute of Technology.

Winton has received numerous literary honours, including being shortlisted for the Booker Prize and becoming the first person ever to win the Miles Franklin Literary Award four times – one of which was for *Cloudstreet*.

In addition to his much-lauded adult novels and short stories, Winton has published books for children including the Lockie Leonard series, the fable *Blueback* (1997) and picture books like *The Deep* (1998) and *Jesse* (1989). Several of his novels have been adapted for the screen, and *Cloudstreet* is also a successful stage play.

Cloudstreet is Winton's fifth novel. Much of it was penned in an outdoor cafe in Paris. Some time later, the completed handwritten manuscript was left behind on a train in Rome, to Winton's utter dismay. A stranger ran after him, handing it back. This unlikely situation seems to reflect perfectly the underlying question of the protagonists in *Cloudstreet*: is life all merely chance, or is there some other explanation for events?

Synopsis

Cloudstreet depicts the lives of two families thrown together, apparently by chance, after separate family tragedies. The Pickles family inherits the Cloud Street house, with a clause in the deeds disallowing its sale for 20 years. They manage to maintain ownership of Cloudstreet despite Sam Pickles' terrible luck with the bookies. But Sam's gambling necessitates the taking in of paying tenants in order to keep the family from starvation. Enter the Lambs, who have suffered unspeakably after the almost-drowning of their son, Fish, which left him with severe mental impairment for the rest of his life. Their loss is palpable, as Fish's condition strips a 'Godfearing' (p.26) family of their former faith. For some time, they appear to be simply existing, without hope and utterly devoid of joy.

The two families live side by side awkwardly for 20 years, each inhabiting half the house. They evade each other for the most part, avoiding lengthy conversation, keeping their relationship businesslike. The three Pickles and six Lamb children grow up barely knowing each other, despite sharing a bathroom.

Sam continues to have good and bad luck at the races – mostly bad – and his wife, Dolly, steadily declines: drinking heavily, regularly being unfaithful to Sam, and losing her looks and her will to live.

Oriel and Lester Lamb work in their grocery shop, a converted front room of the huge house. The only respite from their labours comes in the form of occasional fishing excursions, and their involvement at the Anzac Club – where Lester satisfies his vaudevillian yearnings and Oriel serves supper, both of them unwittingly substituting patriotism for God.

Meanwhile, the children grow up – the Lamb girls procuring boyfriends and the Pickles boys living hedonistically (prioritising their own pleasure). The reader is privy to Quick Lamb's and Rose Pickles' perspectives and we sympathise with Quick's agony and misplaced guilt over Fish's inability to grow up, and with Rose's increasing hatred of her mother and her general unhappiness, manifest in anorexia. Quick runs away to the country where he shoots kangaroos for a living and tries to find a clear sense of purpose for his life. Rose is a conscientious and intelligent student and does not want to leave school but, at her mother's insistence, goes to work on the switchboard at Bairds, a Perth department store. On the phone at work she meets Toby, a self-professed 'intellectual' who further undermines her self-esteem when she goes out with him.

For Oriel, Quick's leaving is effectively the loss of a second son, since Fish no longer recognises her as his mother since his 'drowning'. In her grief, she works her family into the ground, determined to run any opposition in the area out of business. Her success in this goal causes her no joy, however, and she is forced to say sorry for the first time in decades. Lester has one brief sexual encounter with the promiscuous Dolly, which leaves him feeling guilty. He then helps Sam out of a few tight situations with the 'union men' who come to collect on their losses, and an unlikely friendship develops between the two men.

Quick returns to Cloudstreet and, unaccountably, he is glowing. One night out in the boat on the river he comes across Rose sobbing. They talk, haltingly but meaningfully enough to realise that there is love between them. Their marriage would appear to be the quintessential 'happy ending', uniting the two families, but Winton characteristically refuses to resolve the story so simplistically. Quick enters the police force, a means by which he hopes to become the 'good man' he knows himself to be. Rose miscarries and begins to starve herself again.

It is obvious at this point that things are coming to a climax. Resolution can only occur after a catharsis and here it must take the shape of forgiveness. Dolly tells Rose why she has been so bitter and Rose finally understands her mother's slow path to destruction. She can now carry a pregnancy successfully and – as her name suggests – with it, she blooms. The birth of Rose and Quick's baby, Harry, is the glue that finally binds the families together and even Dolly resolves to be a good grandmother.

The denouement of the story brings it full circle: Fish returns to the water which had almost claimed him 20 years before, and which had been calling him home all these years.

Character summaries

The Pickles family

Sam Pickles: ex-guano miner; works at the Perth Mint; gambles, especially on horses.

Dolly Pickles: wife of Sam; mother of the three Pickles children; alcoholic; cheats on her husband; consumed with despair for much of the novel.

Rose Pickles: (b.1935) works at Bairds department store; marries Quick Lamb in 1959; gives birth to Wax Harry in 1963.

Ted Pickles: marries and moves away; becomes a jockey; dies in sauna.

Chub Pickles: (b.1936) remains at Cloudstreet.

The Lamb family

Lester Lamb: (b.1894) husband of Oriel; father to the six Lamb children; ex-policeman and farmer, now works in and cooks for the Cloudstreet grocery shop.

Oriel Lamb: (b.1901) ex-farmer; works in Cloudstreet shop; married to Lester and mother to the six Lamb children; lives in a tent in Cloudstreet's backyard for much of the novel.

Hattie ('Hat') Lamb: marries Geoffrey Birch.

Elaine Lamb: Hat's twin sister; suffers frequent headaches; has a long engagement but doesn't marry by the novel's end.

Red Lamb: (b.1932) tomboyish and stubborn; becomes a nurse.

Mason ('Quick') Lamb: (b.1934) becomes a police officer; marries Rose Pickles with whom he has a son, Wax Harry. Note that although 1934 is the birth year for Quick that is most consistent with the novel's events and time frames, it is inconsistent with the facts that Quick is two years older than Fish (p.27), and that Fish was born in 1933 (p.341).

Samson ('Fish') Lamb: (b.1933) 'drowned' at age nine but revived by his family; suffers brain damage from the incident and never grows beyond a mental age of about five.

Logan ('Lon') Lamb: (b.1939) marries Pansy with whom he has two children.

Minor characters

Aboriginal man (unnamed): sporadic, unannounced visitor and gentle, mysterious adviser to the inhabitants of Cloudstreet; a kind of prophet/angel character.

Toby Raven: frustrated writer and quasi-intellectual; Rose's boyfriend for a brief time, to whom she loses her virginity.

Lucy Wentworth: farmer's daughter who seduces Quick in the wheat belt; the discovery of their tryst eventually forces Quick to leave the area.

Beryl Lee: lonely war-widow who meets Oriel at the Anzac Club and is invited to live at Cloudstreet. Beryl works in the Lambs' shop and after some time leaves to become a nun.

The 'Nedlands Monster': based on an actual serial killer (Eric Cooke) who preyed on young women in the early 1960s in Perth; eventually caught, tried and executed.

The Cloudstreet house itself: experiences feelings and memories; responds to the pain and joy of its inhabitants.

BACKGROUND & CONTEXT

Cloudstreet is a rambling novel of epic proportions, spanning about 20 years and encompassing World War II (1939–45). The story opens in the northern coastal town of Geraldton and a southern coastal town, both in Western Australia, in 1943. In these settings the reader learns of the two central families' motives for coming to Perth to live in the huge house that becomes known as 'Cloudstreet'. Literally, the Lamb and the Pickles families come from opposite directions and meet in the middle, establishing the metaphor for when they come together emotionally at the novel's close. Although the families leave the coast and come together in the house, water (whether the Indian Ocean or the Swan River that leads to the sea) is a metaphor for life in this novel, and it is pivotal to the families' epiphanies that they not stray too far from it.

Politics

Politically, the narrative voice is sympathetic towards the working class and displays some antipathy towards those who exploit them. Robert Menzies, Prime Minister from 1939 to 1941 and again from 1949 to 1966 (most of the period covered by *Cloudstreet*), is an arch-conservative referred to as 'that bastard' (p.156) and not afforded any sympathy in the novel. Sam feels that there is little point voting, as the political party of 'tightfisted boss lovers' (p.405) has been in power for so long. However, more left-wing political sympathies are not exactly lauded, either. Sam notes:

> There's two other things people say are worth believin in – the Labor party and God, but they're a bit on the iffy side for my money. The ALP and the Big Fella, well they always got what I call a tendency to try an give ya what they think ya need. (pp.101–2)

Sam regards the Menzies establishment as 'the enemy' and yet 'the big knobs of the union didn't seem much different … You'd never pick em for workers, not in a month of Sundays' (p.156). In his own small way he gets back at them while he works at the mint: 'There weren't many coins bigger than a peppermint and it was easy to take something out now and then for the kids ...' (p.157). The narrative voice regards this small crime with sympathy, encouraging the reader to do the same.

The world beyond the house

Quick is profoundly affected by John Hersey's novel *Hiroshima* (1945), introduced to him by his history teacher. It makes him aware of the scale of the tragedies outside his own life, of which he was previously ignorant. At 16, Quick becomes vaguely aware of the Korean War (1950–53) in the context of Australia's increasing affiliation with the United States and gradual disassociation from Britain. Despite this awareness, the residents of Cloudstreet seem to be, for the most part, preoccupied with their own survival. To Quick and Rose's generation, World War II is little more than an abstract idea, no more significant than 'the foot of a Jap soldier washed up in a twotoed rubber boot' (p.19). To an extent, this asserts the 'tyranny of distance' and resulting apathy felt by Australians in the generations following the world wars. Although Quick's self-flagellation can hardly be called apathetic, it is largely self-absorbed.

The novel also suggests a context of the 'corporate cowboy culture' which Winton has often condemned in interviews and which, in resource-rich Western Australia, became prevalent after World War II. The natural world and a sense of history was (and is) sacrificed to successive mineral booms and the resulting urban 'shopfronts'. This necessitated the tearing down of historical buildings, the destruction of the natural landscape and the exploitation of resources by those 'trying desperately to hit the big time' (p.289). Feelings of regret and anger over the destruction of the landscape are sometimes expressed by the characters in *Cloudstreet*. For example, Oriel is nostalgic for the country she once knew:

> Out there ... they're bulldozin streets and old places, fillin in the river, like they don't wanna leave any traces behind. I reckon Harry'll never see the places we know. Can you imagine that? (p.411)

Race relations

The novel deals with relations between black and white Australians during the period covered by the narrative (the 1940s through to the 1960s). Sam's surprise that the Aboriginal man he meets on voting day – and Aboriginal people generally – do not have the vote in the mid 1960s is significant. It demonstrates white Australia's ignorance of the plight and place of Aboriginal Australians at the time. Sam's shocked realisation: 'Jesus ... paint him white and he might be me old man' (pp.405–6) jolts him into some understanding and fellow-feeling. Rose's knowledge of Aboriginal disenfranchisement at least gives some hope for the following generation's relative enlightenment. The Aboriginal man's gentle, bemused cynicism certainly makes him a sympathetic character. Even if he is not able to vote, he is able to joke with Sam about politics: 'Only the bosses don't know theys the bosses, eh' (p.405). Although in his interaction with Quick he seems preoccupied with the importance of home and belonging, he is drawn as a wise and sensitive man rather than a person embittered by two centuries of dispossession.

Capital punishment

Society's changing attitudes towards capital punishment are also highlighted in *Cloudstreet*, and it was only a few years after the novel's setting that the last person was executed in Australia. When Quick reads in the newspaper that the Nedlands Monster is to hang, Oriel's opinion is a clear indication of where the narrative sympathy stands on the death penalty:

> Killin is men's business, [Oriel] said, not God's. If you think it's somethin to celebrate leave God out of it.
>
> ...
>
> What about an eye for an eye and a tooth for a tooth?
> Barbarism! snarls Oriel. That's for primitive tribes. (p.395)

Quick also expresses sadness over the fact that the man is not granted his simple, final wish: to be buried next to his little son who had drowned.

GENRE, STRUCTURE & LANGUAGE

The prose style of this novel is very lyrical, with ebbs and flows reflecting the omnipresent water which is always at the centre of the narrative. Direct speech is minimalist, reflecting the characters' relative inarticulateness, and speech marks are not employed, integrating direct speech with the third-person narrator's observations. A number of features of the novel's structure and language contribute to this sense of fluidity and of emotional and spiritual dimensions to everyday physical realities. These are discussed in detail in the following sections.

Structure

Within the novel's 10 chapters, the narrative is broken up into vignettes or 'windows' to the action or to the soul of a character. Some are very brief, even a single paragraph, and others are much longer. Several of these segments have symbolic titles alluding to Christianity, such as 'Disciples' and 'Fatted Calf'; others are simple descriptors such as 'Summer' and 'The Pig'; others take their titles from words or phrases contained within them. Literary critic Nancy Vittorin-Vangerud likens the novel's structure to the movement of the ocean:

> There is more bounty, more possibility for us in a vista that moves, rolls, surges, twists, rears up and changes from minute to minute ... The sea is the supreme metaphor for change. (2002, p.2)

Narrative point of view

The narrative is made up of brief moments of interior monologue and third-person 'windows' into the motives and inner workings of the characters. At times, Fish is the first-person narrator in his heightened perspicacity (insightfulness). There is a God-like quality to Fish's narrative in his capacity to see into the very souls of his family members: some of whom, like Oriel, he cannot connect with in his temporal or everyday 'earthly' life. The other sections of narrative represent a kind of enhanced omniscience, told in the third person and focalised through various characters, with the perspectives of Rose, Quick, Sam and Lester most prominent. Other characters are revealed predominantly through their actions and occasional conversation.

Fish is actually more than one character, in the sense that his levels of awareness are different in the temporal (earthly) and the eternal (spiritual) domains of his life. His eternal dimension is effectively put on hold while he lives out a temporary everyday existence at Cloudstreet, helping, unbeknownst to them, to bring about not only the eventual synthesis of the two families but the integration of the temporal and the eternal within the people he loves. When this happens, towards the close of the novel, Fish's 'work' in the temporal sphere is complete: the narrative voice observes, 'Your time will come, Fish, you'll have a second of knowing, a man for a moment, and then it won't matter because you'll be me ... free of the net of time' (p.179).

Even God appears to have a voice in the narrative, which seems audacious but in this context it does not offend as blasphemous:

> Soon you'll be a man, Fish, though only for a moment, long enough to see, smell, touch, hear, taste the muted glory of wholeness and finish what was begun only a moment ago ... The earth slips away, Fish, and soon, soon, you'll be yourself, and we'll be us; you and me. Soon! (p.420)

There is also an internal focalisation evident in *Cloudstreet*, where the narrative has access to what characters think, feel and see, over and above that which is tangible and visible. An example of this style is the final commentary from Fish: 'I burst into the moon, sun and stars of who I really am. Being Fish Lamb. Perfectly. Always. Everyplace. Me' (p.424).

The inability to communicate

In Winton's work many of the characters are thwarted to some extent by their inarticulateness. Winton is all too aware of the (particularly masculine and Australian) incapacity for talking openly about intense emotion. He has said that:

> People have terrible yearnings and feelings. They know what they think and they know what they want to say, but they just don't have the words. It's not so much the vocabulary; the words are in their throat, but they're not on their tongue ... (Willbanks 1991, p.195)

This idea is represented in Winton's literature through the device of omission, which is employed by an author to enhance readers' understanding of relationships. The characters' incapacity to relate and to connect is reflected in the way that much of the dialogue between characters is stilted and inadequate. However, at certain times the characters find ways to overcome the distance and silence between them. This is evident when Rose and Quick learn how to talk and catch up on their lives, telling each other their innermost secrets once forgiveness has occurred, as well as when Dolly discovers a capacity to unburden herself, all in a rush out on the back step of the house with Rose (p.357).

Humour

Humour plays a vital part creating balance in a story replete with tragedy and despair. There are many examples of humour in *Cloudstreet*. Oriel fantasises about the sign that could be placed outside their shop if they were as ostentatious as their competitor, 'G. M. Clay – Ex 2nd AIF':

> O. Lamb
> [...]
> Married to fool
> Please help ... (p.148)

Another amusing moment is when Sam is 'saved' from a vengeful man by the timely arrival of Lester, fresh from cutting up ham bones with a 'bloody meat cleaver'; Sam seizes the opportunity and cries: 'He's a mad bastard – be careful. Look at this, for Chrissake!' and then holds up 'his stump and the man's eyes grew in his face' (p.189).

The language is often scatological (or amusingly crude), which also adds humour to the novel's realism, such as when Dolly comes upon Oriel in the backyard dunny:

> I'll go and get the ranger …
> Smells like something's crawled up inside you and died.
> The door slapped shut.
> NO WADING. (pp.77–8)

Another example of crude humour in the novel is Red Lamb's great 'method' for discouraging the boys from spying on her in the change sheds at the baths: 'she could piss right into their awestruck faces while bellowing her war cry "Death to Pervs!" She could pee through the eye of a needle, Red Lamb' (p.127).

Light-hearted humour with a gently irony is noticeable with Sam's acquisition of Stan the cocky, who eats new pennies:

> When those coins dropped out of him onto the kitchen table two days before Christmas, he cocked his head at all present. He fixed his eyes on them with irascible turns of his head.
> Eh? he said. Eh? What?
> Stan always paid his way. (pp.88–9)

Imagery

The story is heavy with metaphor and symbol. The use of imagery is often linked with the use of humour, such as in the following metaphor:

> [Lucy] put him through a few manoeuvres that ended in a long, stalling climb which had Quick Lamb shuddering at the point of blackout. Then she abandoned the controls altogether and left him dusting crop at high revs. (p.203)

However, there are also more profound and extended metaphors throughout *Cloudstreet*. An example of such powerful imagery is one which uses an old negative stereotype regarding Aboriginal Australians – that of addiction to cheap wine – and turns it around. When Quick runs from the wheat belt and the scandal with Lucy Wentworth, he encounters the 'blackfella' thumbing a lift. The man offers him, Jesus-style, the two (symbolic) tangibles of the Christian Holy Communion:

> From his gladstone bag the stranger takes a bottle and a loaf of white bread.
>
> Whacko, says Quick.
>
> The black man pulls him off a hunk of bread and Quick takes it. Then the bottle. It scourges his mouth. It takes everything he has not to spit.
>
> What is this stuff?
>
> Muscatel, the black man says. (p.209)

Following this Eucharist-in-transit, the man directs Quick, mysteriously, home to Cloudstreet, getting out of the car near the house and saying 'Comin?' (p.210). Quick is so chilled by the man's knowledge of where he lives that he flees again for over a year, representing a rejection of the path he knows instinctively to be the right one. But, as the narrative always suggests in *Cloudstreet*, it is never too late. Quick's rejection is symbolic of humanity's general rejection of its eternal potential: 'He did not think of home, but home thought of him' (p.212). The black man has Messiah-like qualities, such as when he is seen 'walking upon the water' (p.217). Quick first observes, then dismisses, these qualities with scepticism. When he first sees the man on the water he thinks, 'He was black ... But everyone's black at a distance', and he then becomes apprehensive: 'Quick pushed past him and didn't look back' (p.217).

Water symbolism

The redemptive symbolism of water is called upon to illustrate epiphany (enlightenment) for various characters. The baptismal (biblical) and evolutionary (biological) journey of Fish Lamb towards the water recurs in the lyrical prose. The water metaphor in Winton's fiction often suggests an existential choice: to drown, to drift, to swim against or with a current, to sail, or to founder. As critic Nancy Vittorin-Vangerud puts it:

> Australians are surrounded by ocean and ambushed from behind by desert – a war of mystery on two fronts. Of the two mysteries, the sea is more forthcoming; its miracles and wonders are occasionally more palpable, however inexplicable they may be. (2002, p.2)

The sky and the sea are fundamental to *Cloudstreet*, as with most of Winton's other fiction. They are inextricably linked:

> … and when Quick looks over the side he sees the river is full of sky as well.
> Are we in the sky, Fish?
> Yes. It's the water.
> What dyou mean?
> The water. The water. I fly. (p.114)

The strength of Fish and Quick's bond is such that they have momentarily drifted beyond the current of time and the particularities of place. They are in a state in which 'Heaven' is not 'divided' from earth.

There is an overarching theme of connectedness within the novel, conveyed largely by the imagery. The Pickles family resides alongside the Lamb family: the two names suggest a meal of roast lamb with pickles as a common condiment. Significantly, such a combined family meal occurs towards the novel's end, the imagery suggestive of the Last Supper with its ending and new beginning.

Binaries

Winton uses a wide range of binaries, or opposites, in his writing. He is also aware of the necessity for integration of such opposites. His writing emphasises the importance of bringing things together in a spirit of reconciliation.

Dualisms (another word for opposites or binaries) occur regularly within *Cloudstreet*, the most common being that between the rational (easily explainable with logic) and the non-rational (unable to be explained logically) worlds. One of Winton's creative missions in the novel is the integration of these two elements. As critic Veronica Brady puts it, 'he takes us across the boundaries of experience where mere "facts" refuse to go' (cited in McGirr 1999, p.43). Acceptance of the inter-relationship between the material (temporal) and the supernatural (eternal) worlds poses less of a problem for the characters who are given the greatest opportunity to express their inner lives, namely Sam, Rose, Quick and Fish. These are the sympathetic characters who readers feel closest to, and whom they care most about.

Personification

Personification (endowing inanimate objects with character human traits) is employed in this novel through the house-as-body known as Cloudstreet. The house is often described as experiencing sensations and emotions just as a human character might. For example, 'Outside, it was a summer's day. The house twisted its joists, hugging inwards, sucking in air, and the two women wept together on the sagging bed' (p.357).

This is a feature that demonstrates the inextricability of person and place, the significance of home in people's lives and the necessity of belonging somewhere. The house feels the pain and joy of its inhabitants and the characters are affected by the house, particularly by the sadness incarcerated in the library.

CHAPTER-BY-CHAPTER ANALYSIS

Prologue (pp.1–3)

This lyrical and intensely sensuous opening is related from an omniscient narrator who the reader comes to recognise later as Fish Lamb himself. Then, in Chapter 10, it becomes apparent the entire story of *Cloudstreet* has taken place in this initial, pivotal moment of the narrative, 'those seconds it takes to die, as long as it takes to drink the river, as long as it took to tell you all this' (p.424).

Q Who is the 'us' mentioned in the prologue?

Q What indicators are there that this novel will have a spiritual element?

Chapter 1 (pp.7–22)

Summary: *The Pickles family is introduced in Geraldton; Sam injured on a boat; Dolly unfaithful; Sam inherits a house in Perth from his cousin.*

The Pickles family is introduced in this chapter. Sam works out on the Abrolhos Islands collecting guano for superphosphate. One day, while 'hauling birdcrap' (p.12), Sam's right hand is caught in the cable and he loses his fingers. He is airlifted to hospital in Geraldton and while he is recovering Dolly sleeps with the American pilot, cursing her lot in life and berating Sam for being 'useless' (p.16).

After the accident Sam, Dolly and the three children – Ted, Chub and Rose – live in and help run a Geraldton pub owned by Sam's cousin Joel who, while out fishing one day with Sam, has a fatal heart attack. (As Sam is Joel's only relative, he inherits not only money, but a ramshackle house in Perth that Joel had bought after a win at the races, and Sam feels his own luck changing. This is revealed in Chapter 3.)

Q What are the dynamics in the Pickles family?

Q What does the reader learn of Dolly, Rose and Sam and their relationships with each other at this point?

Chapter 2 (pp.25–32)

Summary: *The Lamb family is introduced; they go prawning on the south coast of Western Australia; Fish Lamb becomes entangled in the net and almost drowns; Fish is revived by his mother and the family believes it is a miracle, but Quick knows there is something wrong with Fish.*

The reader is introduced more literally to the Lamb family, and their regular habit of prawning down by the water on the south coast of Western Australia. They are 'Godfearing' (p.26), salt-of-the-earth farming types: Lester, Oriel and their six children.

This chapter tells of the 'drowning' of Fish in the net when Lester and the two older boys are prawning in the dark, and it describes the equally horrifying revival Oriel performs on him on the beach. The family races back into town to the church to give thanks for the miracle, only to discover later that Fish is brain-damaged from his time underwater and will retain the mental capacity of an infant all his life.

Being close to his brother, Quick knows before the others do that all is not right with Fish.

Key point

The tragedy with Fish is the turning point in the Lambs' relationship with God and provides the catalyst for their move to Perth.

Q What has actually happened to Fish?

Q What impressions of the Lamb family are given before the accident?

Chapter 3 (pp.35–80)

Summary: *The Pickles family moves into Cloudstreet; Sam gambles the money he inherited; the Lambs answer the Pickles' advertisement for tenants; a doctor suggests Fish should be institutionalised; Oriel's difficult and tragic life before marriage is described; Lester joins the Army band; Quick is consumed with guilt over Fish.*

The Pickles family moves into the enormous house in a beachside suburb of Perth and Rose is delighted with all the space, apart from the library which is inhabited by several spirits. One is of an early owner of the house, who took in 'native' girls with missionary zeal (p.36). The other is the spirit of one of her charges: an Aboriginal girl who suicided in despair at being parted from her family and mistreated in the house. The room exudes sadness. This is the first indication that the house has its own character.

In addition to the house at Number One Cloud Street – later simply named 'Cloudstreet' – Sam also inherits £2000 which he promptly gambles away, necessitating the advertisement for tenants. The Lamb family sees the advertisement and moves in to the other side of the house from the Pickles. Two families could not be less alike.

Quick is brought undone by Fish's condition and his own misplaced guilt over the incident. He feels he should have been more vigilant and able to extricate Fish from the net. In his tormented state he sticks pictures of refugees and people ravaged by war and starvation on his wall, ensuring that an awareness of others' suffering is always present in his mind.

This chapter also marks the introduction of the unnamed Aboriginal man into the characters' lives: a man selling kindling door-to-door. Lester invites him in but he disappears after stepping one foot in the house. The implication is that he senses something sinister in the house that the others are yet to articulate.

Q How do the descriptions of Oriel's past life affect the reader?

Q How is the house described?

Q What is happening to Quick emotionally?

Chapter 4 (pp.83–134)

Summary: *World War II finishes; Sam and Lester become friends after Sam takes Lester to the races; Lester buys a small boat with his winnings and Quick and Fish row it back to Cloudstreet from Fremantle; Sam loses more money gambling and Dolly declines further; Oriel cleans up after Dolly and the two women and Rose become more estranged; a bonfire on Guy Fawkes night goes wrong; Sam wins a pig that talks, and gives it to Lester; Oriel moves outside into her tent.*

With the war over, life settles into a routine at Cloudstreet. Things are not always easy, but there are moments of comedy amid the bleakness, such as when Sam brings home a swearing cocky named Stan, adding some 'light relief' to the story. The contradiction of Sam winning a job at the Perth mint from a game of two-up is similarly amusing.

Sam and Lester strike up an unlikely friendship and Lester, 'corrupted' by Sam, gambles at the races for the first time in his life. Oriel is incensed but still joins the family when Lester, on a high from his win, takes the family fishing. In Fremantle, Lester impulsively buys a boat without considering how they will get it home. Quick volunteers to row it all the way down the river and asks to take Fish with him. Although dubious and frightened, Oriel and Lester realise Quick needs to prove himself responsible for his brother. The boat has not arrived by dark and the family is desperate, but Quick and Fish get back in the early hours.

Key point

On this journey down the river, the closeness between the two brothers is evident, as is Fish's yearning to return to the water. There are parallels with their previous shared water experience, but this time Quick is able to bring Fish home safely.

The financial and emotional strains on the Pickles family begin to impact on the Lambs too, and on the families' relationships with each other. Sam's luck takes a downward turn again and he begins to sell some of his family's belongings. Dolly's drinking is so out of control that one night in a violent rage Oriel has to clean up after her and extends her domestic frenzy into other parts of the Pickles' half of the house. This shames Rose and makes Dolly despise Oriel even more vehemently.

When the two families share a Guy Fawkes night celebration, some kind of peaceful and even companionable coexistence seems briefly possible, but the evening quickly unravels when Fish cannot bear the sight of the burning effigy – whom he confuses with Jesus – and Quick is embarrassed, in front of Rose, by his father's animal impressions.

Sam wins a pig in a raffle and gives it to Lester who plans to fatten it up to eat. Fish, however, informs his father that the pig can talk and that he, Fish, understands its language. Lester, with his gentle, world-weary cynicism, sees the irony in this: 'Always the miracles you don't need' (p.130). Soon after this, Oriel moves her bedding and a few personal items outside to a large tent. Her motives are speculated upon wryly by the onlooking neighbours.

Q How is the relationship between Oriel and Dolly depicted?

Q What is the significance of the pig?

Q Comment on the signposting in this chapter of future relationships.

Chapter 5 (pp.137–92)

Summary: *Quick's despair and guilt make him more depressed and he leaves Cloudstreet for the country; Oriel is distraught and begins her campaign against the shop's competition; Rose becomes thinner, starving herself, then is forced to leave school and gets a job in a department store; Beryl Lee comes to live at Cloudstreet.*

This chapter sees Quick leave Perth for the wheat belt of Western Australia in an effort to purge himself of all that has long been troubling him; his 'sadness … radar' (p.89) is so over-sensitive that it is making him ill. The final straw for him is his teacher's disappearance from school directly after having revealed to Quick information and graphic illustrations about concentration camps. There is a suggestion that Mr Krasnostein himself, or members of his family, survived a concentration camp. Quick takes this personally, believing his own membership with and enjoyment of the army cadets, and his youthful ignorance of suffering on such a scale, has offended his teacher and driven him away.

When Quick leaves, Oriel is distraught at losing another son (she feels Fish's 'loss' palpably, since he cannot seem to relate to her at all) but instead of grieving in any conventional way, she resolves instead to drive G. M. Clay and his nearby grocery store out of business. The ramifications of this do not dawn on her until Oriel, having won her little victory, visits Clay's deserted wife who has been left with no financial support. Oriel, uncharacteristically, feels terrible remorse over this and Rose is amazed one day to see her crying 'Like a person' (p.173). As though to appease her conscience over the war over ice-cream that ruined the Clays, Oriel brings the war-widowed Beryl Lee home from the Anzac Club. Beryl boards at Cloudstreet and helps in the shop.

Rose continues to fade away and this worries Sam who tries in vain to force her to eat. Dolly, in her callous approach to her daughter, simply forces her to leave school and get a job. Rose does, reluctantly, operating the switchboard at Bairds department store. She gradually begins to enjoy the camaraderie of the girls at Bairds, and gains some weight.

Ted Pickles leaves, much to Dolly's chagrin as he is her favourite. It is revealed that he has run away because he has made a girl pregnant.

Q Why does Oriel become fanatical about G. M. Clay?

Q Why is Beryl brought back to Cloudstreet?

Q Why does Quick feel he needs to run away?

Chapter 6 (pp.195–220)

Summary: *Quick culls kangaroos for farmers; Quick hallucinates about Fish; Quick has a sexual relationship with farmer's daughter, Lucy, and when discovered has to leave in a hurry; Quick works for his uncle driving trucks for a year; he meets the Aboriginal man who hints that he must go home, and has a truck accident which forces this to occur; Quick arrives at Cloudstreet 'glowing'.*

In the wheat belt Quick lives a solitary life, culling kangaroos for a farmer. He sleeps in his truck, a dog his only companion – although he has a kind of telepathic communion with Fish, and dreams often. One day he is injured and in his delirium he is nourished in spirit by Fish who seems to call out to him across the paddocks.

Quick is rescued by the farmer, who takes him back to the house where Lucy, the farmer's daughter, seduces him shamelessly and subsequently manipulates him into a sexual relationship in which he has no interest. They are discovered and, in disgrace, Quick leaves the area for good. He heads south and runs into his uncle who gives him a job driving a truck.

On the way to his uncle's he meets up with an Aboriginal man who materialises as though from nowhere and then appears again, months later, following an accident with the truck after which Quick takes a break to go fishing. Quick is puzzled by the man and is overwhelmed by the feeling that he must go home. After his accident, Uncle Earl and Aunt May drive him home to Cloudstreet where he arrives, inexplicably 'giving off a light' (p.219). Fish, it transpires, knew he was coming hours beforehand.

Q What happens to Quick, spiritually, out in the wheat belt?

Q How can the reader account for Quick's glowing?

Q What is the significance of the Aboriginal man's appearances?

Chapter 7 (pp.223–73)

Summary: *Hat gets married; Lester has sex with Dolly; Lester takes Sam away to escape the men to whom he owes money; Beryl warns Lester about Dolly and later leaves Cloudstreet; Quick finally recovers and goes prawning with his mother where they discuss Fish's drowning and what their obligations are.*

Quick arrives back in Cloudstreet on his sister Hat's wedding day. In this chapter Lester offers to pay off Sam's debts. Spontaneously he has sex with Dolly and somehow Beryl Lee knows, warning him to stay away from Dolly.

Feeling a sense of guilty obligation Lester secrets Sam away to a shack in the bush to avoid the debt collectors and their threats. Soon after, Beryl leaves Cloudstreet, confessing to Lester that she is in love with him.

Quick recovers from his strange affliction and he and Oriel go prawning together, finally talking honestly about what happened to Fish years before. They agree that they are all partly to blame for the tragedy and owe him a decent life.

Q Why does Lester commit adultery and how does he feel afterwards?

Q How is the relationship between Sam and Lester depicted in this chapter?

Chapter 8 (pp.277–321)

Summary: *Rose has a relationship with Toby Raven; Rose runs from Toby, realising they are too different; Rose encounters Quick and Fish in the boat on the Swan River and joins them; Quick and Rose talk and eventually go back to Cloudstreet where they make love in the library.*

Rose reaches a crossroads in her life, meeting Toby Raven at work and losing her virginity at the age of 24. Toby is an aspiring but hitherto thwarted writer. At first Rose feels honoured by his attentions but she gradually becomes aware of their disparate social standings. Finally, when Toby – humiliated at a party in an affluent home – insults Rose, she leaves him and runs to the river. Here she finds Quick and Fish, out for a row in the dark. She joins them in the boat and she and Quick talk while Fish sleeps.

They realise they belong together, and return to Cloudstreet where they sleep together in the library. They are married six weeks later.

This event, and more specifically the site of the library, is significant as it is a symbol of the reconciliation of the two Cloudstreet families. The domestic reconciliation also hints at a redemption of sorts for colonial European atrocities against Aboriginal people; a conflict represented by the events in the library years before.

Q Why does Rose know Toby to be wrong for her and Quick to be right?

Q What does Toby expose about another way of life?

Chapter 9 (pp.325–85)

Summary: *Rose and Quick move out; Quick joins the police force and helps as they attempt to foil a serial killer; Rose has a miscarriage; Ted Pickles dies; Dolly succumbs to despair and goes missing briefly; Rose is persuaded to come to Cloudstreet and care for Dolly; Dolly tells Rose why she has been so bitter and forgiveness ensues; Rose and Quick move back into Cloudstreet; Rose has a baby, Wax Harry, on the same night as the Nedlands Monster is captured.*

Rose hankers to live in one of the new suburbs springing up around Perth, and they combine her pay from Bairds, extra from taking in ironing and Quick's income from his new job with the police, to save for a State Housing house. The Nedlands Monster is at large and Quick is desperate to track him down, which links to Quick's sensitivity to suffering, and his desire to stop 'evil' in the world (p.366). Rose miscarries and begins starving herself again.

The death of Ted Pickles drives his mother to absolute despair and, violently drunk, she goes missing. When she is found, Rose is persuaded to come and care for her at Cloudstreet and she does so reluctantly. The catharsis for Dolly occurs at this point. Dolly reveals to Rose that she has been incapable of loving her all these years because she herself was the victim of abuse by an older 'sister' who was actually her mother. Rose begins to forgive Dolly for the first time and, as if the two things are directly related, Rose's health is restored and soon after she becomes pregnant again, this time carrying the baby successfully.

On the beat one evening Quick meets the Aboriginal man yet again. Unbeknownst to Quick, this man's timely appearances are catalysts for him to return home. Quick and Rose move back to Cloudstreet, ostensibly because the Nedlands Monster is still on the loose (even the usually strong Oriel feels vulnerable outside in her tent) but really they are returning because they know it is where they belong.

The killer is eventually caught – on the same night that Rose gives birth, with both families looking on and helping out at the birth. The baby is called 'Wax' Harry because, as Quick observes, he looks waxy when newly born. One of the properties of wax is to meld things together, and symbolically this baby is what reconciles the two families after 20 years of awkwardness, resentment and contempt. Dolly resolves to be a good, if unconventional, grandmother, perhaps making up for some of her failings as a mother.

Q What purpose(s) does the inclusion of a real murderer have?

Q How does the birth of Harry affect the various family members?

Q What indicators are there, early in the chapter, that something momentous will soon happen?

Chapter 10 (pp.389–426)

Summary: *Quick, Rose, Wax Harry and Fish all go camping in the country; Quick makes a link between Fish's drowning and the drowning of the Nedlands Monster's son; the Nedlands Monster is hanged; the Pickles family has owned Cloudstreet for 20 years and considers selling; the two families decide to stay on, including Rose and Quick; both families have a picnic at the river and Fish wanders off, drowning completely this time; Oriel folds her tent and moves back inside.*

Quick, Rose and baby Harry prepare to take a family holiday but Fish is desperate to come – perhaps thinking of the last time Quick abandoned him. They finally agree and the four of them go on a holiday east into the West Australian countryside. Just prior to their departure, Quick pulls the Nedlands Monster's drowned young son out of the river and this affects him profoundly, as it is so reminiscent of the old tragedy with Fish. He unburdens to Rose, as though free to speak meaningfully for the first time.

The requisite 20 years of ownership of the Cloudstreet house is reached and Sam vaguely considers selling up but decides against it, partly due to the intervention – once again – of the Aboriginal man with his gentle wisdom.

The two families have a great picnic down at the river and this time Fish wanders off unnoticed and drowns completely, returning to the water at last. This fulfils a strong desire Fish has held through the text – the desire to be one with the water – with the implication that the interruption of his first death was more curse than blessing for Fish, leaving him incomplete. In his last moments, Fish is finally able to 'recognise [himself] whole and human' (p.424).

After Fish's death, one short section remains to close the novel. In a symbolic gesture of acceptance, reconciliation and homecoming, Oriel and Dolly together fold up Oriel's tent in the backyard.

Q Why does Sam decide not to sell Cloudstreet?

Q What does the reader learn about social attitudes of the 1960s?

Q Symbolically, what does the folding of the tent suggest?

CHARACTERS & RELATIONSHIPS

Winton's characters are not always sympathetically portrayed. Many of them are hopeless or even repulsive and the social and physical landscapes within which they operate are often oppressive and demoralising. There are thematic challenges for the reader in the temporal world the characters inhabit and Winton himself is often reluctant to interpret them outside his texts. But he does say:

> the world is a bigger, weirder, more elastic place than we sometimes like to think. The only miracle is that things aren't worse, that people aren't twice as rotten, that we're still plugging away. For the moment ... (cited in McGirr 1999, p.99)

Sam Pickles

Key quotes

'Don't try to be cruel to her, Rose. She's had her chances, she's nearly finished. Winnin out over someone like that isn't much of a victory ... Whatever I'm gunna get in this life I've had, and damnnear all that's been lost ... Christ Jesus, when yer family goes after it, it's more than a man can bear.' (p.348)

'To be alive, to be feeling, to be conscious. It was the cruellest bloody joke. In the dark, night after night, he raised his mangled fist to the sky and said things that frightened him.' (pp.161–2)

Sam Pickles is a loving man, and though his irresponsibility with money is destructive to his family (what a gorgeous irony that he works at the mint!), his unwavering devotion and innate wisdom eventually discourage both Rose and Dolly from slow but persistent suicide.

Sam has a religious soul, believing with absolute certainty in the existence of a power higher than himself. To an extent this makes him passive, conveniently blaming his bad luck on such a higher power, as though he were simply an onlooker in his own life. However, it also makes him grateful for the things he has: for family and for life itself.

Sam (the name is derived from the Hebrew, meaning 'God hears') has a fatalistic faith in the 'Shifty Shadow', otherwise known as 'Lady Luck' or the 'Hairy Hand of God', that deals out arbitrary judgements on humanity.

His eternal optimism even in the face of the fickle Shifty Shadow, while obviously irritating to his family, is refreshing in an often bleak narrative: 'Expect bad luck, was his new creed, and now and then you'll be surprised. It saved him from a lot of disappointment' (p.188).

Sam's love for Rose and for Dolly is a constant in their lives that they do not often appreciate due to his inconsistency as a provider. He is by nature open to love and accepts his place in the family and in his workplace. Sam could be dismissed as a weak character, easily led and with hopelessly addictive tendencies, but for his consistent faithfulness. He never loses conviction that the spiritual realm is very real, however random he deems it. This consciousness is sometimes his undoing: Sam's doubt as to whether he or something supernatural is in control of his life can lead to an abrogation of responsibility, which often means he loses all his money (see pp.161–2).

Dolly Pickles

Key quotes

'Garn, ... you'd tear me bloody eyes out if I didn't come with a feed, wouldn't you? ... Well, you gutless wonders! You'd eat ya children!' (p.373)

'It was like they were electric with all knowledge, all places, all people ... She never did get to try those rails.' (p.79)

Dolly is both self-destructive and injurious to others. Despite her looks, she has no self-esteem and the dreadful reason for this is revealed just in time to effect a reconciliation with her daughter, something the reader would not have imagined possible through most of the narrative. Her childhood, we discover late in the narrative, was one of incest and abuse, resulting understandably in self-loathing. She is a nihilist (negative; despairing; hostile to common beliefs about life having meaning) for most of the narrative, slowly suiciding with the aid of alcohol and inertia. Only when she opens up to Rose, realising she is almost too late for redemption within her family, does she find some meaning and a capacity to love.

Dolly is undeniably a home-wrecker in her own home, an observation articulated by her son Ted:

> Reckon it's a friggin house o cards, I do ... The old girl's the wild card and the old man's the bloody joker.
> Sam surprised them, coming up behind. There was blood dripping from his nose. (p.41)

Dolly is also a wrecker of others' stability. A betrayed wife in the neighbourhood implores Sam to try to harness his wife:

> You don't know me, and I really don't know you ... but I think you should try to control your wife ... It's my husband I'm talking about. I've got youngens to look after and she's got no right. It's a mortal sin! (pp.157–8)

Dolly believes nothing holds meaning beyond the transitory, and her life is an uneasy combination of pleasure-seeking and self-abuse. Her hatred of her only daughter is creating a third generation of abuse and despair. Dolly's own history is one of instability, suggesting the cyclical nature of destructive patterns. She was uprooted from Geraldton where she 'was somebody, she meant something' (p.42). Her doll-like looks are fading and her heavy despair has reduced her to becoming an escapist from life itself, wanting to go anywhere the train tracks near her home might take her but never having the courage to take that journey. Her thoughts sometimes impose themselves upon the narrative, such as when she sits by the railway, reflecting upon life's unpredictability (p.79).

Dolly's experimentations with alcohol and sex are simply transitory acts empty of deeper meaning. While her alcoholism could be perceived as gradual suicide, it does not represent an irrevocable loss of hope and when Ted – her favourite child – dies, she becomes aware of what literary critic Sahlia Ben-Messahel calls 'her own otherness' and she 'desperately tries to settle things down' (1998, p.67). Her eventual transcendence over her despair, through her own will and determination, illustrates Winton's disdain for nihilism that continues indefinitely. There is a suggestion within the tone of the narrative that if someone like Dolly can decide to save herself from the void of absolute denial to break destructive patterns, surely anyone can. She is even able to see an irony in her own enlightenment, seeing her past self reflected in the marauding magpies on the back step (p.373).

An important and quite refreshing aspect of Dolly's epiphany is that she does not change her personality, becoming sweetness and light. Rather, she is still essentially the same:

> Dolly bitched and whined about everything until Rose began to realize that half the time the old girl was bunging it on – she was play acting just to amuse herself. Sure, there was still heat in the old battleaxe, but not much of an edge. (p.358)

Key point

Dolly's transformation is a very naturalistic one – it is subtle and believable rather than extreme and spectacular. This contrasts with other more fantastical or magic realist elements of the novel, such as Quick's glowing or even Fish's resurrection.

Lester Lamb

Key quotes

'Maybe he didn't go along with it anymore, but he sure as shillings couldn't get out of believing in it.' (p.102)

'I used to be crippled with stories … loaded and hopeless with em. Now I can't work up a decent joke.' (p.191)

Lester is a loving man, generally an optimist despite the tragedies of his life. He loves his family and has an innate sense of fun. It pains him that he no longer believes in God, or at least that he finds it difficult to believe. 'The Fish thing' (p.60) has left the entire family rudderless, but while Oriel is furious with God, Lester feels His loss sorely. He throws himself into the Anzac Club by way of compensating. Here he finds a sense of belonging and of fulfilling a patriotic duty following the triumph of the Allies in World War II. (He does not appear to recognise the irony of this, given that 8000 Anzacs did *not* return from Gallipoli in World War I.)

Lester also gets into the spirit of a spinning knife game to determine, for example, who does the washing up. The Lambs say that the 'knife never lies' (p.53), and despite Oriel's objections that it is a 'heathen' activity, even she is amused by it (p.53). This family habit is often repeated throughout the story and Lester finds himself wondering if chance is all there is. He feels guilty for even thinking this, but life has been cruel and readers can sympathise with his loss of faith.

The narrative supports an understanding of such people who may have rejected God, perhaps unwillingly, due to tragic circumstances. There are suggestions throughout that the Lambs will never quite rid themselves of God, no matter how vehemently they denounce him. Lester cannot discard a lifelong faith so easily, and he introspectively observes that he can't 'get out of it' (p.102).

Lester works hard in the shop but is not obsessed with labour in the same way his wife is; he would far rather be out fishing with the family.

Oriel Lamb

Key quotes

'Since Fish … I've been losin the war. I've lost me bearins.' (p.231)

'She loved Lester, but a lot of loving him was making up for him, compensating.' (p.95)

'A winner wins them all, Lester, not just the worldly things.' (p.230)

Oriel is superficially a hard case, her family secretly referring to her as the 'Sar'major'. The reader learns that in her past she has had a difficult life with little affection shown to her, bringing up her father's new family after her mother's death and losing a loved half-brother to the trenches of World War I. Her earlier life with Lester was one of eking out a meagre existence on a farm in south-western Western Australia, bringing up their six children.

Part of her likes frugality. Oriel takes pride in her ability to make something out of nothing, to patch and scrape and save. Her work ethic is fierce and she believes her whole family should be equally conscientious. She regards herself as the strength of the family and believes men in general lack 'some basic thing', although she isn't sure what (p.95).

Key point

For Oriel, life is 'all war' (p.229) and a war she feels she must win. But in a rare moment of shared introspection, Oriel admits her alienation to Lester when she says she feels she's losing that war (p.231). She knows the material (or temporal) world is not enough, despite her position of relative financial security and respect in the community.

Although Oriel is severe, she also has another side. Oriel has a depth of compassion that surfaces in odd but still practical ways, such as the taking in of a complete stranger: the widowed and desperately lonely Beryl Lee. Beryl needs a home, a family around her and something to do. Oriel recognises this and, ever-pragmatic, benefits from an extra pair of hands in the shop, knowing that she is about to lose a daughter to marriage.

Oriel's faith changes throughout the novel. She has been religious all her life but has little tolerance for God once ' ... not all of Fish ... had come back' (p.32). Fish's resuscitation appears to be a miracle until his brain damage becomes apparent. Oriel tries to become thoroughly self-sufficient, and she appears harsh and judgemental to her family. She sets herself above and apart from them, eventually pitching a tent in the backyard where she sleeps every night. She is torn apart by Fish's lack of recognition of her but will admit this to nobody, throwing herself industriously into making the shop the best within miles, and wondering 'if it wasn't really the way things were, everything just happening by chance in this sorry world' (p.56). When she attends her daughter's wedding, Oriel keeps '... her eyes off the Christ pictures, the ones that really set her teeth. It was like fighting off a toothache – you had to concentrate and will, overcome, pretend, become another thing' (p.227). Paradoxically, at one point, Oriel reprimands Quick for using the Lord's name in vain.

Oriel disapproves vehemently of Dolly's bad mouth, loose morals and sloppy apathy, while Dolly for her part despises Oriel for her assumed superiority and straight-laced frigidity. Oriel does not ask Dolly (or Sam) to call her by her Christian name until after 20 years of their acquaintance (unlike Lester, who had crossed this bridge with Sam years before). As a result, the final scene of the novel is very poignant, representing the breaking down of a seemingly impenetrable fortress of disdain between the two women. This suggests that reconciliation is possible even under the most unlikely circumstances.

Mason (Quick) Lamb

Key quotes

'... he is alive, he is lucky, he is still healthy, and his brother is not ... Fair dinkum, Quick Lamb hates himself.' (p.61)

'Every important thing that happened to him, it seemed, had to do with a river. It was insistent, quietly forceful like the force of his own blood.' (p.300)

Quick, the eldest son of the Lamb family, is burdened for the majority of the story with misplaced guilt over the 'drowning' of his brother Fish. Quick experiences an unbearable sense of 'banishment, his quiet punishment for the Fish thing' (p.60). His inability to even articulate the event refers back to Winton's comment that sometimes 'people just don't have the words' for what they want to express (Willbanks 1991, p.195). Quick's sense of survivor-guilt becomes heightened to the point where he assumes culpability for a 'blinded prisoner of war or a crying baby or some poor fleeing reffo running with a mattress across his back' (p.61). After Fish's near-drowning, Quick is old enough to witness the change in his parents, from devout churchgoers to apparently Godless fatalists, and he predicts that faith 'wouldn't come for any of them anymore' (p.94).

At high school Quick is challenged by his (Jewish) History teacher regarding the human cost of war, and again feels guilty for his ignorance and his naive enjoyment of the Army cadets. The teacher gives Quick several magazines, and Quick finds inside them 'loose photographs of what looked like burnt logs or furniture, but when he looked close he saw the features of people ... It was called *Belsen: a record*' (pp.139–40). His teacher's failure to appear at school the next day confirms Quick's perception of himself as an agent of harm.

Feeling he must escape the torment and avoid bringing about any more tragedy, Quick embarks on a lonely and aimless odyssey into the

West Australian wheat belt where he can lose himself in hard work and an endless landscape with few distractions. Yet even here Quick is besieged by his guilt; it comes to him in hallucinatory dreamscapes where he still cannot save Fish, yet somehow Fish now seems in charge, on a mission, such as when Quick sees him 'rowing' a fruit box across the wheat:

> You goin home, Fish?
>
> The Big Country.
>
> The box rights itself again … He's too damn big for a fruit box. He looks bloody stupid, that's what, a man rowing a crate. Across the wheat. (p.201)

Quick's epiphany is brought about by the love and spiritual insight provided by Fish; the Aboriginal man who appears at critical points to dispense wisdom; and the memory of the omnipresent river. Quick reflects on the confluence of his narrative and the river: 'Every important thing that happened to him, it seemed, had to do with a river' (p.300). Quick is also guided by the gentle wisdom of his father Lester, who, when Quick says he has no ambition other than to be a 'good man', reminds his son that this is hardly difficult when there is little to challenge him: 'Easy to be a good man out here – there's no one else to think of' (p.304). This is accepted by Quick who soon after becomes a compassionate and useful member of society.

Rose Pickles

Key quotes

'Everything, you stole from me. Even when I was a teenager you *competed* with me, your looks against mine. Shit, even my grief you steal from me. You can't imagine how I hate you.' (p.352)

'… Rose got thinner every day. The old woman went into rages and the old man bit his lip. She was sixteen and scaring herself.' (p.143)

'Rose felt things falling within her, a terrible shifting of weights.
My God. My God. Mum!' (p.357)

Rose is embittered for most of the novel, hating her mother with good reason; we could possibly read Rose's anorexia as a weapon that she uses against her mother as a form of punishment. She feels that her childhood was denied her, having learnt too early about human vices; she recalls overhearing her mother and another man in the pub 'snorting and snouting like … but I'm a girl, I don't know this' (p.349). She also resents being expected to cook and clean for her dysfunctional parents and brothers. But she is shown to have a depth of compassion when her mother's catharsis occurs towards the novel's end and reconciliation becomes a possibility.

Intelligent and astute, Rose is a good student who does not want to leave school but, once forced to, she begins to enjoy the camaraderie of the other girls on the switchboard. Amazingly, after all Rose has been exposed to since childhood, the girls manage to shock Rose with their bawdy humour.

Rose is infatuated and fascinated by Toby Raven, her first beau, but she realises he is not for her: 'We're different, said Rose' (p.287). The night she runs from Toby into the arms of Quick is an example of dramatic irony in the sense that the reader can see it coming long before Rose herself can. Her blindness to this inevitability is part of the novel's exploration of the characters' resistance to their need for a 'homecoming' (physical, emotional and spiritual).

Rose's bitterness eventually spills over into her marriage and seems to be feeding off itself, resulting in a miscarriage and palpable despair: 'She felt like she was made of steel' (p.338). Finally she allows forgiveness to override her bitterness.

Samson (Fish) Lamb

Key quotes

'Wait, Oriel, keep strong Mum, keep the steel, you'll see. Oh, how I missed you all my life. You'll see it's best this way. Wait.' (p.397)

'… I feel my manhood, I recognize myself whole and human, know my story for just that long, long enough to see how we've come, how we've all battled in the same corridor that time makes for us, and I'm Fish Lamb …' (p.424)

While the narrative is primarily third-person in *Cloudstreet*, Fish's perspective shows a heightened perspicuity (compassionate insight) and his stream-of-consciousness voice acts as a refrain, to ground and gently inspire the reader. The inclusion of the brain-damaged, childlike Fish as a pivotal voice is a confirmation of humanity: an affirmation that all life is of value. Fish, while still loved and accepted by those around him, is affirmed as an individual more through his discourse with the reader than with characters in his own reality, despite his efforts to reach his frenetic family (see p.397).

It seems paradoxical that Fish Lamb, thwarted in his expression more than any other character (due to his brain injury), is a narrator in *Cloudstreet*. He is, along with the old Aboriginal man who fades in and out of the narrative, the character who draws the others' attention to the spiritual realm. His heightened sensibility is manifest in the miraculous, and in his quiet observations, when the world and all its hopelessness and ugliness intrudes. As Winton observes of Fish, his 'is the controlling intelligence of the narration, yet intelligence is, presumably, what he lacks' (cited in McGirr 1999, p.56). Fish resembles characters in biblical narratives whose intellectual handicaps mark them as having been 'touched' by God. Fish's ability to communicate 'in tongues' with the pig in the backyard (p.131) is presented as the (albeit useless) miracle it is, elevating him to a status beyond the temporal world. However, he is still very much a part of that world. This is indicated when, as a grown man, he soils his pants during the camping trip in the wheat belt.

Fish is of the water in a primeval sense. Our biological beginnings, many believe, are in the water and perhaps we need to reconnect, just as all the earth's water is connected. The narrative suggests this need in a conversation between Fish and Lester:

> Yeah. And the water. Yairs. They go in the water. To the big country. Yeah.
>
> [...]
>
> An people there for em, says Fish. There's people there.
>
> Oh, God.
>
> Fish looks smiling upon him. (p.192)

At the novel's close when Fish returns – running – to the water for good, Quick recognises the necessity of it and 'makes himself stop' before he catches up to Fish (p.423). The place where Fish is headed is not just the water, but where sky and earth meet, where the temporal and the eternal are in synthesis.

Minor characters

The Aboriginal Man

Key quotes

> 'Go home ... This isn't your home. Go home to your home, mate.' (p.362)
>
> 'You shouldn't break a place. Places are strong, important ... Too many places busted.' (p.406)

Though Winton has publicly professed a Christian belief, the representations of such in his work are unconventional. Aboriginal spirituality sits comfortably alongside Protestantism in *Cloudstreet*. While remaining faithful to a Christian ethic, the narrative voice is influenced by other spiritual possibilities alongside, it appears, a recognition that the possibilities may not be mutually exclusive. As Winton has observed, 'Everything has its place in communicating the grace of God' (Salter 1987, p.10).

Through Quick, and to an extent through Fish, readers are made aware of the Aboriginal prophet. He serves as a conscience of the people; as critic Bruce Bennett puts it, he is a 'guardian angel who is rejected ... the guy is saying: Learn to belong, don't break community' (Bennett 1991, p.63). The man's unexpected appearances in characters' lives at times when they are spiritually bereft are met with fleeting curiosity, mystified fearfulness (as when the man bafflingly knows where Quick lives) or indifference. Only towards the novel's end do the characters discuss the Aboriginal man with each other.

This man also personifies a narrative stance that is incensed at the treatment of Aboriginal people in white Australia and the ignorance of those who do not give it a thought. For example, when they meet on voting day, Sam does not realise that the man does not have the vote even in 1964, and his reaction is: 'Jesus, that's a bit rough, isn't it? They need a union' (p.411).

The Nedlands Monster

The inclusion of the 'Nedlands Monster' (an actual serial killer in Perth at the time of the novel's setting) as a character in *Cloudstreet* is more than simply a device for locating the novel historically; he is a symbol of forgiveness by way of Quick Lamb. Quick recognises humanity's universal fall from grace, 'it's not us and them anymore ... It's us and us and us' (p.402). When caught, the description of the criminal is quite sympathetic: he is 'just a frustrated man with a hare lip who's gone back to his lifetime of losing, and the pathetic sight of him robs the detectives of the feeling they'd expected' (p.381). The fact that the murderer is not granted his dying wish to be buried alongside his dead son evokes within the reader a degree of compassion for the murderer.

Toby Raven

Toby is an aspiring writer who has had nothing but literary rejections when he meets Rose. Rose is fascinated by him, probably because, being educated and articulate, he is so unlike anyone she has ever met. But she knows he is from a different world and that their relationship is unsustainable in the long term. Toby is the man with whom Rose loses her virginity and this is important for her sense of womanhood. Her self-esteem is damaged at the party to which Toby takes her to celebrate having a manuscript accepted but Rose, by refusing to stay, asserts her self-worth. It is significant that she runs from Toby and recognises that Quick is the man for her on the very same night, suggesting that her escape to the river and Quick's presence there is somehow preordained rather than coincidental. Toby is astute enough to recognise that Perth is a 'Philistine fairground' (p.289) yet not introspective enough to recognise that he too is inauthentic and shallow at this point in his life.

Lucy Wentworth

Although minor, Lucy is an important character in that she represents a diversion from the direction in which a main character is destined to travel. Quick has a brief dalliance with her in the wheat belt where he is effectively running away from home, his conscience and his own entelechy (personal potential). She is an unwitting catalyst for his return home and so, although Quick has no lasting interest in her whatsoever, she is important to the narrative.

Beryl Lee

Beryl is a desperately lonely widow whose husband went down with his military ship. When Beryl turns up, destitute, at the Anzac Club, Oriel takes pity on her, exposing an uncharacteristic compassion. Charity, though, is necessarily tempered with pragmatism for Oriel, and Beryl pays her way, proving a hard worker who is an asset to the Lambs' commercial endeavours. Beryl is a good-hearted woman whom the Lamb girls see as slightly pathetic but she has a depth of passion which she confesses to Lester. In order to quell the desire for someone she cannot have, and obviously needing to belong somewhere, Beryl, a devout Catholic, decides to become a nun.

Discussion questions about characters and relationships

Q How do Oriel and Dolly reach an understanding?

Q Why does Lester need Sam as a friend and vice versa?

Q Is Rose and Quick's relationship destined, and why or why not?

Q What does Fish indirectly teach various family members?

Q What purposes do the minor characters serve in the novel?

Q Why is each family important to the other, both practically and symbolically?

THEMES, IDEAS & VALUES

It is important to understand that themes – or representations of facets of humanity and society – are rarely, if ever, to be considered in isolation. All the following themes and ideas are interrelated, further endorsing the concept of 'connectedness' that underpins *Cloudstreet*.

God, faith and belief

Key quotes

'Thy rod and Thy staff they comfort me, a bit of [Quick's] brain said, Thy rod and Thy staff ...' (p.213)

'What about the Bible, Mum, that's your old inspiration isn't it? ... I've seen you out there with it, burnin the midnight candle.' (p.395)

'Because, look, even the missing are there, the gone and taken are with them in the shade pools of the peppermints by the beautiful, the beautiful the river.' (p.2)

The Lamb family is first described as 'Godfearing' (p.26) but their faith is sorely tested when Fish 'drowns', especially since they initially believe his resuscitation to be a miracle, then discover that it isn't – at least not completely. Theirs is a simple, unquestioning Christian faith until this turning point. But for both Oriel and Lester, relinquishing God is awful and not simply because old habits die hard. They question whether or not God is there at all, and if so, whether He is as benevolent as they had always believed. Oriel still has a Bible outside in her tent and the suggestion is that she reads it habitually every night, even if she is angry with God. She is unfulfilled and unhappy, although would never admit it, and there is an underlying suggestion in the narrative that she will never be happy unless reconciled with God.

Lester does not hate God. It is as though he has lost a friend on whom he had always relied. He misses believing and part of him is loath to let it go altogether. He plays the knife game with the children, commenting jovially that 'The knife never lies' (p.53). Interestingly, it is Fish who shouts these words out most enthusiastically and yet he is the one who, on his elevated spiritual plane, is apparently closest to God – an angel of sorts. Perhaps this represents a proposal within the narrative that people should not take such superstitious practices seriously; that they are games and nothing more. Lester wonders if, in fact, chance is all there is, and is not heartened by the possibility, but rather seems saddened. The fact that he wins on his first ever bet but does not subsequently make a habit of gambling is evidence of his possible disillusionment with the notion of chance.

Sam Pickles believes in a supernatural dimension but rather than it being a personal relationship with a creator, Sam believes this metaphysical power distributes good and bad luck arbitrarily. He does not appear to think good luck is allied with his own good deeds, or bad luck with bad deeds. For Sam, luck is utterly random, but thoroughly omnipotent (all-powerful).

Dolly, on the other hand, is completely nihilistic – not showing any belief in deeper meanings or powers – until she forgives herself and others, and is finally forgiven by those closest to her. Redemption, then, is available even to those who eschew religious belief or faith. The narrative suggests, through the metaphor of families living side by side in this suburban microcosm, that all types of people need each other: the religious, the lapsed believers, the secular, the agnostic, the superstitious – all must connect to each other to arrive at truth.

The perspicuity of the Aboriginal angel-prophet shows Winton's capacity to embrace other spiritual narratives alongside a Christian one. The insight of this man who appears whenever someone needs to reconnect with home (as when Sam briefly considered selling the Cloudstreet house, or when Quick is far away) is significant to the narrative. He is unassuming, polite and has no grandiose pretensions. He is simply *there* and the inhabitants of Cloudstreet give him little conscious thought, despite being vaguely puzzled by his materialising at particular times and places imparting gentle reminders.

The importance of religion and belief is evident in *Cloudstreet* not just through various characters' attitude, but also in the symbolism on which Winton chooses to focus. For example, the baptismal property of water, with its symbolic capacity to wash away sin, is a religious trope (idea) and is ever-present throughout the narrative. Fish himself, in his connection to water, is also an example of religious symbolism. Reconciliation of the Lambs to God seems inevitable, with Fish as a catalyst and a prophet of sorts; even his name is important, redolent of a secret symbol of Christianity in fifth-century Rome, based on the New Testament image of Jesus as the 'fisher of men'.

Family, connectedness and belonging

Key quotes

'I'm in this old house with the boy next door and his baby, and I'm not miserable and starving or frightened. I'm right in the middle. It's like a village, I don't know.' (pp.418–19)

'... it would save all kinds of embarrassment if a gesture was made, a compromise sealed, and they ate together.' (p.408)

'There they all are, the Lambs in Lester's lovely old Gothic and it seems right and just. We're here, Oriel thinks, calm again; we're here orright.' (p.333)

The narrative suggests that family life is central to human wellbeing. Dolly's dreadful early experience of family life has scarred her almost irrevocably (note the almost) and the pattern of destruction continues into her own family with disastrous results. Once she acknowledges, with some remorse, her daughter's hatred, she is confronted with the 'old question ... Bad mother, or no mother at all? Christalmighty, she should know the answer to that one by now' (p.175). Her conviction at this point is that to have no mother would be better, having suffered so much at the hands of her own. Yet this is eventually contrasted with the fact that Rose needs her in so many ways. Although Rose appears to give up on her mother many times, her anorexia and emotional detachment are cries for help, endorsing the notion that even Dolly is better than no mother and that there is always hope. Dolly compensates late but not too late, reconciling with Rose and deciding she will make up for lost time with her grandson. This endorses the narrative's argument for the importance of family.

Sam would have lost the house a thousand times over were it not for the clause against selling within 20 years of the inheritance. The family's meagre possessions come and go, according to his run of luck. But his love is steadfast and, despite Dolly's infidelity and abusiveness, Sam never gives up on her. This is so significant as to override all else, although it is often not appreciated. When Rose happens upon her father with the razor poised to cut his throat one day in the bathroom, she is jolted into a recognition of Sam's importance to the family.

When – utterly distraught over the death of her favourite child, Ted – Dolly goes missing and is finally found, Rose bitterly refuses to go and minister to her. She asserts her independence, metaphorically attempting to wash her hands of her mother, saying to her husband, 'God, Quick, I'm married. I'm my own person' (p.351). But Quick intuitively knows she must go to help, that she is really the only one to do it. If she did not, the reconciliation that allows them to move forward could not occur.

The Lambs are disconnected in their own ways: Oriel's move outside to be apart from her family; Lester's adultery; Quick's decision to run away to the interior of the state; Lon's contemptuous dismissal of Fish and his retardation. Despite these fractures within the family, Lester works hard to keep the Lambs united. He organises fishing outings, reprimands Quick for forgetting Fish on occasion and tries to get to the bottom of Oriel's anger. He doggedly maintains a sense of fun even at the most trying times. Eventually this is shown to be a salvation for the family: Lester is the peacemaker and moderator, keeping the fraying edges of his family from unravelling completely.

The Aboriginal man who fades in and out of the narrative serves to instruct characters about their need for family, but his reminders are routinely forgotten. The fact that his gentle remonstrations are often overlooked, and that decisions are arrived at as though the Lambs and Pickleses themselves had thought of them, is representative of the way that much of humanity has overlooked the lessons of history generally and that European Australians have overlooked and marginalised Aboriginal people and their culture.

A strong example of the narrative suggesting the value of family and belonging is Rose's return to Cloudstreet. Rose finally comes to realise the significance of home and rejects the new house in the suburbs that is being built for them. Interestingly, though, she does not appear to recognise this enough to articulate it until she is at a distance from it, on the camping trip in the wheat belt.

The significance of place

Key quotes

'Places are strong, important.' (p.406)

'A house should be a home, a privilege, not a possession.' (p.410)

'There's no home as specialized as mine, Mister!' (pp.67–8)

The unnamed Aboriginal man serves to remind the characters of the importance of place, just as he does with the importance of family. Sam meets him soon after voting, and the black man's gentle warning that no-one should 'break a place' affects Sam profoundly (p.406). Sam's enthusiasm for making money from possible future developers of the Cloudstreet site suddenly wanes. During this interaction, Winton also illustrates two fundamentally different conceptions of place and belonging. The Aboriginal man says to Sam, 'You live there', referring to Cloudstreet, and Sam's reply is: 'Yeah. I own it' (p.405). This is a familiar representation of the difference between Aboriginal and European relationships to place.

The importance of home is explored in the younger generation of Lambs and Pickleses too. The new house Rose desires following her marriage, and for which she and Quick save so earnestly, is portrayed as a sham – it is all about appearances and is dreadfully lonely, so that eventually they are drawn back to Cloudstreet again to bring up their child in the bosom of the family. The physical closeness of the people in the house is a metaphor, of course, for emotional closeness. Only in these circumstances can the kind of conversations that Dolly has with Rose occur, from which forgiveness and new beginnings can emanate. After Harry's birth, Quick and Rose are tempted by the idea of independence and talk about moving to 'the scrubbed bricks, the dinky letterbox, the planted lawns' of the suburbs (p.404). However, they are lonely for Cloudstreet and never actually move into the new house.

Domestic spaces within houses can be as important as the house itself. The library at Cloudstreet is an example of a significant and symbolic place. Tragedies occurred in that room years earlier (when an unpleasant European woman ran the house as a mission for Aboriginal girls) and the repercussions are felt until the novel's present, because redemption or healing has never occurred. It is ironic that it was a priest who suggested the taking in of Aboriginal girls to teach them skills for domestic work in white homes. The subsequent suicide of one of these girls, and the other girls' misery, highlights the often misguided altruism of the church, and suggests a European arrogance over Aboriginal people's traditional understanding of the importance of place and family. The room itself is sad – the past has affected it – until it opens up to new life when Harry is born, and history is redirected.

Place in *Cloudstreet* refers not just to homes but also to the environment. An enduring motif is that of water and its redeeming capacity, so that whenever characters stray too far from it they feel alienated. The trip Quick and Rose and Fish take into the wheat belt once they have all connected is shown to be a safe diversion, since there is certainty that they will return home. On the other hand, when Quick goes by himself in late adolescence to escape his home (and its inherent association with water), it injures him, body and soul.

Loss, grief and the power of forgiveness

Key quotes

'Oh, Mum. You never told me. You never ever said. Don't cry, Mum. Please.' (p.357)

'I know how that poor bastard feels. And I got thinkin about my childhood, my life. I did a lot of feelin sorry for myself, those years. I used to see the saddest things, think about the saddest, saddest things.' (p.402)

'All down the street you could hear them singing, those mad buggers from Cloudstreet, sounding like a footy match.' (p.412)

'The little boxy woman and the big blowsy woman folded end to end till the tent was a parcel ... and then they went inside the big old house ...' (p.426)

One of the prominent characters who must learn to forgive before her own epiphany can occur is Rose Pickles. She is bitter for the majority of this story and has good reason to be, since effectively she has lost her childhood and grieves for what could have been. Dolly has been emotionally cruel to her, has not set her any positive examples and Rose has had to bring up herself and her brothers. She appears callous at times yet the reader understands that this is a protective shield she has constructed around herself for survival. Sam attempts to provide Rose with an example of forgiveness, in his everyday life with Dolly, but for much of the narrative Rose scorns this as weakness on his part.

But it is obvious that Rose cannot sustain these feelings, especially when she sets about starting her own family. The very moment Dolly unburdens to Rose the reasons for her incapacity for love, forgiveness is forthcoming and appears to be an overwhelming relief for both Rose and Dolly. Not only does Rose begin to forgive her mother, but Dolly can, at this point, forgive herself. It is as though she has just made the connection between her past and her own actions. Rose's successful pregnancy that immediately follows is a kind of benediction and opens a new chapter of hope.

The Lambs also have to forgive God. This may seem an outrageous proposition but it is mandatory they do so in order to effect their own healing. Oriel in particular has a hard time of it and when the reader resists a disdain for Oriel's obsessive, stern superiority and considers what she has suffered, some sympathy can be extended to her. Her life has been a succession of losses, beginning with her mother, and leading to the emotional loss of Fish, which seemed to be one loss too many for her to bear.

Oriel, like Rose, has built up an impenetrable wall and will not admit to any vulnerability. It smarts that Fish does not even recognise her as his mother but it does not seem to occur to her that Fish cannot possibly connect emotionally with her while she herself is so 'closed off'. Again, as with Rose, such stoicism is not sustainable; something has to give. Forgiveness again is the key but, for someone like Oriel, it might seem like a loss of face. So it is inevitable that her forgiveness of God, and her forgiveness of her own stubborn denial and lack of love, do not happen until the novel's close.

It is significant that on one family picnic to the river Oriel ties Fish to a tree, knowing his yearning to return to the water, although not understanding it. However, at the combined family picnic at the novel's close, nobody restrains Fish and the family does not even notice him walking off to the water. This could be read as a tacit acceptance that Fish belongs somehow to the water and to the otherworldliness it represents; that he is, indeed, called to return to that spiritual dimension.

Nationhood and Australian identity

Key quotes

'This is the country, and it's confused. It doesn't know what to believe in either. You can't replace your mind country with a nation, Lest. I tried.' (Oriel, p.232)

'... his vote hadn't done the country a stick of good ... those tightfisted boss lovers would be back for another term, sucking up to the Queen and passing the hat round to the workers again ...' (p.405)

Although *Cloudstreet* has an international appeal (evidenced by its having been translated into many languages), it also makes some subtle statements about what it means to be Australian, and about the socio-political direction in which Australia seems to be heading. For example, after their marriage, Quick and Rose reject the new suburbs in favour of moving back to the infinitely more attractive ramshackle house at Cloud Street. This indicates a somewhat romantic attitude towards the value of the older country houses and a bygone era. In the 1950s and 1960s Perth had begun to spread with alarming speed, further away from the water onto sandy inland areas, spawning depersonalised suburbs with no soul or character. Other Australian cities are following suit to this day. *Cloudstreet* offers a commentary on the changing nature of Australian residential culture. The Anzac Club, where Oriel and Lester retreat after their rejection of God, proves to be no substitute for home. Instead of finding their grace manifest in family, the Lambs keep looking outward and there is a sense that they are trying too hard to make it work. There is no mention of Lester and Oriel forming any genuine friendships out of this club: even Beryl Lee is initially a charity case who becomes a convenient live-in help in the Lamb's shop.

The narrative presents a sceptical attitude towards power and those who wield it, an attitude which is identifiably Australian in both its irreverence and its unpretentiousness. Despite the Lambs' advance payment of their rent, Oriel still maintains that 'it does you good to be tenants. It reminds you of your own true position in the world' (p.410). Here, Oriel recognises that the temporal life, however tragic, is transitory and that in an eternal sense we are only ever tenants. Similarly, Sam's justifiable fear of the 'union men' shows the standover, mafia-style tactics employed by the very institutions supposedly established to support the working class at this time. Sam describes how he owes money to his boss, or to 'One fella who owns all the fellas', and says he'll be able to pay him back because 'There's plenty of shonky jobs they'll want done' (p.234). When Dolly asks him, 'Haven't you got some union mates to back you up?' Sam replies with a smile that 'They are the union' (p.234). Lester is less tolerant, recognising them for the 'grovellin bullies' (p.235) they are.

There is a natural Australian egalitarianism endorsed by the narrative. The working class is celebrated for its tenacity and perseverance in this novel, especially in the face of myriad disappointments and a lack of disability benefits. Despite the difficulties of their lives, however, those in the working class are loyal to their own culture and there is no respect for the upper classes nor for so-called democracy. Toby Raven's delusions of grandeur and the arrogance of affluent partygoers at the house in Dalkeith where Toby takes Rose hold absolutely no appeal for readers. Like Rose, we cannot get out of there fast enough.

It is possible for tenacity and perseverance to go too far; for example, Oriel's obsessive work ethic is portrayed as unhealthy – even destructive – in that it undermines, and leaves little time for, family. On the whole, though, a strong work ethic – such as Lester's approach of a good honest day's work with family at the forefront – is endorsed by the narrative. Lon's lazy attitude and his choice to take a 'sickie off work' (p.399) does not endear him to the reader. We are encourage to applaud Oriel's disciplining of Lon: in front of the entire street full of neighbours, she makes him reload the truck because, as she reminds him, 'We do things a certain way in this family, Lon. It's called the proper way' (p.400). This attitude to work allows the Lambs to have some bargaining power in the Cloudstreet house, because their rent is paid up years in advance, affording security for the family.

The sanctity of life

Key quotes

'There'd been times he'd thought the kid was better dead than to have to live all his life as a child, but he knew that being alive was being alive and you couldn't tamper with that ... life was all there was.' (p.65)

'She ... looked at herself once more in the mirror. All her bones stood out. Her eyes crowded her face. She gave a grim smile and went down to cook the dinner.' (p.141)

'Jesus, Rose, you look like a corpse these days. It's a crime you know, he says quietly, a bloody crime.' (p.159)

Much is made in *Cloudstreet* of the necessity to treasure life, in whatever form it is manifest. This is something Lester comes to accept with relation to Fish and it echoes the situation surrounding Sam Flack's coma in Winton's earlier novel *That Eye, the Sky*, where the family refuses to give up on their apparently brain-dead husband and father. Narrative endorsement comes at the end of that novella when Sam Flack awakens, forcing the reader to concede that it was just as well his life support was not withdrawn.

In *Cloudstreet* as in *That Eye, The Sky*, the narrative suggests that no matter how flawed the human, life is not something man has the right to take away. So, even the evil perpetrated by the Nedlands Monster on innocent women as they sleep in their beds is portrayed almost sympathetically. Quick becomes a mouthpiece for the narrative voice, reminding us that there is always some possibility of redemption; while he is relieved that the killer is captured, he nevertheless recognises that every human harbours the capacity to do wrong.

Rose's emotionally motivated anorexia is portrayed as an unhealthy denial of life, as she starves herself and refuses to value her own existence. Similarly, Quick's youthful obsession with pictures of 'sin and corruption and damnation' is shown to be destructive:

> the saddest, most miserable things he'd ever seen in his life and he kept them there to remind him of Fish, how Fish had been broken and not him. But even that punishment had worn off. (p.140)

The narrative appears to judge such self-abuse (both Quick's guilt and self-blame, and Rose's eating disorder) as futile, and instead values the positive actions brought about by forgiveness. For example, Quick gradually comes to recognise the preciousness of life and the necessity of treasuring it, and this is illustrated by his desire to be a custodian of the community as a policeman. Rose, following her reconciliation with Dolly, is finally able to give birth: an ultimate endorsement of the sanctity of life. The birth of Wax Harry denotes a new chapter uniting the two families and providing hope for the future.

Discussion questions on themes, ideas and values

Q What does the novel suggest about the importance of connectedness and community?

Q What larger idea might the Aboriginal man represent?

Q How does the novel portray Western Australian and, more broadly, Australian society in the 1950s and 1960s?

Q What could be suggested about childhood and innocence in the novel?

Q What does the narrative appear to advocate about forgiveness?

Q How does the novel suggest that faith can be felt, practised and shared in a great variety of ways?

Q How is life (in the sense of being alive) represented in the novel?

DIFFERENT INTERPRETATIONS

Different interpretations arise from different responses to text. Over time, a text will elicit a wide range of responses from its readers, who may come from various social or cultural groups and live in very different places and historical periods. These responses can be published in newspapers, journals and books by critics and reviewers, or they can be expressed in discussions among readers in the media, classrooms, book groups and so on. While there is no single correct reading or interpretation of a text, it is important to understand that an interpretation is more than a personal opinion – it is the justification of a point of view on a text. To present an interpretation of the text based on your point of view you must use a logical argument and support it with relevant evidence from the text.

Critical viewpoints

Most critics appear to be in accord about Winton's creative mission. They agree that he presents characters who, almost without exception, struggle to come to terms with their place in the world, and are often relatively inarticulate in expressing their need to belong and to believe. Belief is something that is individually realised and defined in Winton's characters, despite Winton himself being a fairly orthodox Christian. He acknowledges bemusedly that to identify as a Christian in Australia is 'a real aberration that in the literary culture people will, at best, kind of put up with' (Willbanks 1991, p.196) and an 'oddity in an anti-Christian culture' (Watzke, in Rossiter and Jacobs 1993, p.7).

There are some Christians with antagonistic attitudes towards the depiction of the characters' quests for meaning, one labelling Winton a 'Satanist', with another commenting that 'We [cannot] see the grace of any God worth bothering with' (McPhee 1999, p.24). Generally, though, critics concur that Winton's characters, relationships and situations are refreshingly real; the characters are undeniably flawed but, in Veronica

Brady's words, 'open to infinite possibility, above all to the possibilities of love' (cited in McGirr 1999, p.43).

Winton's characters are quintessentially Australian and become, as critic Anne Day has it, 'surprised by grace' (in Rossiter and Jacobs 1993, p.30) as they do not expect to encounter the eternal in Australia's suburban or rural landscapes which appear so spiritually and physically barren. Yvonne Miels suggests that Winton depicts 'ordinary people [who] celebrate the tough realities of life whilst recognising other immanences' (in Rossiter and Jacobs 1993, p.31). Certainly the sympathetic characters (those the reader is naturally drawn to and who have more of a 'voice' in the narrative) are those who appear to be looking for something outside the everyday sphere and who accept the blessings offered to them in myriad manifestations without 'expecting in that childlike way that there is an answer' (McGirr 1999, p.118). They sense God's presence 'instinctively' and 'within the ordinary' (Miels, in Rossiter and Jacobs 1993, p.31).

The importance of the characters' connections to the landscapes they inhabit (both natural and built) has also been a focus of critical responses to *Cloudstreet* and to Winton's work generally. Roberta Buffi asserts that the vastness of landscape and seascape causes Australians to feel abandoned and estranged, so that they 'try to escape from an alienating city whose physical and moral decay corrupts the urban environment ... and retreat into their contemplation of sky and water' (in Rossiter and Jacobs 1993, p.18). This is especially obvious in *Cloudstreet* where the water connects the characters.

Winton 'reveals his commitment to place', claims West Australian critic Bruce Bennett (1991, p.63), and this commitment is clearly evident in *Cloudstreet* where characters have to go away to recognise their home. As Goonan expresses this, 'if people can stay together as a community and keep battling they will eventually come to believe and belong' (1996, p.97).

Two interpretations

As mentioned in the 'Critical viewpoints' section above, most analyses of Winton's writing foreground his characters' search for something to make their lives more meaningful. As such, the interpretations below are not completely opposed but show how two different critical 'frameworks' or 'lenses' can be used in order to read or interpret *Cloudstreet*.

Reading 1

Cloudstreet demonstrates people's fundamental need to make meaning in their lives.

This statement suggests that the quest for a purpose is essential to a meaningful life. This, in existentialist terminology, is called being authentic. If you think of each character in turn, most in *Cloudstreet* are, even if they are not consciously aware of it, unsettled and destructive without something to believe in and somewhere to belong. Their sojourns into escapist or meaningless directions, such as Quick's time in the wheat belt, Dolly's drinking, Sam's excessive gambling, Rose's anorexia and Oriel's retiring to the tent, are all failed attempts to make meaning or to escape a sense of meaninglessness. As such, at these stages in the characters' lives they are not living authentically since, in their self-denial, they are not acting positively to address their despair and they allow negative aspects of history to repeat through their inaction.

You could ask yourself where the narrative sympathy seems to lie here. Is it for characters who eventually come to recognise that something is missing in their lives and then do something proactive to remove this vacuum? Think, for instance, of Dolly's cathartic unburdening, Rose forgiving her mother, Oriel's folding of the tent and Quick forgiving himself for what he sees as his responsibility for Fish's drowning. Do we as readers want things to resolve for these characters? Do we feel empathy towards them in their very human struggles? What of the characters who appear to live inauthentically, such as Toby Raven – do we feel anything for him? It could be argued that, in this way, Winton steers readers towards a particular world view. Winton's characters are often brutally realistic in order to show that an epiphany – or turning point – is available to absolutely everyone.

It is fitting that *Cloudstreet*'s characters often appear to be hopeless cases. It would be pointless only to have characters whose lives are affluent, settled and comfortable reaching some form of transcendence.

It is the characters' openness to blessings offered and their capacity to act in order to address and overcome their despair that makes them accessible to us.

Reading 2

***Cloudstreet* is intensely religious, rather than Christian.**

As we have established before, Winton identifies as a Christian, albeit an unconventional one. It seems, though, that he does not necessarily fit the description of a Christian writer. This is probably what irritates some Christians (those mentioned in the 'Critical viewpoints' section above who are disdainful of his work). Ask yourself if you feel the novel is didactic (or preaching) in tone. Do you feel Winton is pushing you to view Christianity favourably or as the one correct world view? There is, after all, no suggestion that the protagonists who experience some kind of epiphany towards the novel's close, such as Rose and Quick, Dolly and Sam, actually embrace a life with Jesus at its centre. Their heightened level of awareness seems to be relatively secular, although involving acceptance of elements that are usually associated with religious belief, such as forgiveness, homecoming and appreciation of the sanctity of life. Nor do Oriel and Lester, who were once church-goers (before Fish's drowning), appear to become avidly God-fearing again.

Cloudstreet's mystical element includes a 'Dreaming' type of spirituality, whereby the Aboriginal man just knows about people and their histories, their sorrows and their innate needs. There seems to be narrative endorsement of Fish's Pentecostal interactions, such as his mutual understanding with the pig, on a plane far removed from his old-fashioned parents. There is even a suggestion of primeval belongings, as with Fish's desperate need to return to the water. Consider what effect you think such integration (or connectedness) of different ideas of the eternal has on you as a reader.

Certainly, the substitutes for God like Lester's Anzac Club are shown to be cheap imitations which do not ultimately satisfy. However, *Cloudstreet* suggests that we must all come to our own understandings of what or who 'God' is.

QUESTIONS & ANSWERS

This section focuses on your own analytical writing on the text, and gives you strategies for producing high-quality responses in your coursework and exam essays.

Essay writing – an overview

An essay is a formal and serious piece of writing that presents your point of view on the text, usually in response to a given essay topic. Your 'point of view' in an essay is your interpretation of the meaning of the text's language, structure, characters, situations and events, supported by detailed analysis of textual evidence.

Analyse – don't summarise

In your essays it is important to avoid simply summarising what happens in a text:

- A **summary** is a description or paraphrase (retelling in different words) of the characters and events. For example: 'Macbeth has a horrifying vision of a dagger dripping with blood before he goes to murder King Duncan'.
- An **analysis** is an explanation of the real meaning or significance that lies 'beneath' the text's words (and images, for a film). For example: 'Macbeth's vision of a bloody dagger shows how deeply uneasy he is about the violent act he is contemplating – as well as his sense that supernatural forces are impelling him to act'.

A limited amount of summary is sometimes necessary to let your reader know which part of the text you wish to discuss. However, always keep this to a minimum and follow it immediately with your analysis (explanation) of what this part of the text is really telling us.

Plan your essay

Carefully plan your essay so that you have a clear idea of what you are going to say. The plan ensures that your ideas flow logically, that your argument remains consistent and that you stay on the topic. An essay plan should be a list of **brief dot points** – no more than half a page. It includes:

- your central argument or main contention – a concise statement (usually in a single sentence) of your overall response to the topic. See 'Analysing a sample topic' for guidelines on how to formulate a main contention.
- three or four dot points for each paragraph indicating the main idea and evidence/examples from the text. Note that in your essay you will need to *expand* on these points and *analyse* the evidence.

Structure your essay

An essay is a complete, self-contained piece of writing. It has a clear beginning (the introduction), middle (several body paragraphs) and end (the last paragraph or conclusion). It must also have a central argument that runs throughout, linking each paragraph to form a coherent whole.

See examples of introductions and conclusions in the 'Analysing a sample topic' and 'Sample answer' sections.

The introduction establishes your overall response to the topic. It includes your main contention and outlines the main evidence you will refer to in the course of the essay. Write your introduction *after* you have done a plan and *before* you write the rest of the essay.

The body paragraphs argue your case – they present evidence from the text and explain how this evidence supports your argument. Each body paragraph needs:

- a strong **topic sentence** (usually the first sentence) that states the main point being made in the paragraph
- **evidence** from the text, including some brief quotations

- **analysis** of the textual evidence explaining its significance and **explanation** of how it supports your argument
- **links back to the topic** in one or more statements, usually towards the end of the paragraph.

Connect the body paragraphs so that your discussion flows smoothly. Use some linking words and phrases like 'similarly' and 'on the other hand', though don't start every paragraph like this. Another strategy is to use a significant word from the last sentence of one paragraph in the first sentence of the next.

Use key terms from the topic – or synonyms for them – throughout, so the relevance of your discussion to the topic is always clear.

The conclusion ties everything together and finishes the essay. It includes strong statements that emphasise your central argument and provide a clear response to the topic.

Avoid simply restating the points made earlier in the essay – this will end on a very flat note and imply that you have run out of ideas and vocabulary. The conclusion is meant to be a logical extension of what you have written, not just a repetition or summary of it. Writing an effective conclusion can be a challenge. Try using these tips:

- Start by linking back to the final sentence of the second-last paragraph – this helps your writing to 'flow', rather than just leaping back to your main contention straight away.
- Use synonyms and expressions with equivalent meanings to vary your vocabulary. This allows you to reinforce your line of argument without being repetitive.
- When planning your essay, think of one or two broad statements or observations about the text's wider meaning. These should be related to the topic and your overall argument. Keep them for the conclusion, since they will give you something 'new' to say but still follow logically from your discussion. The introduction will be focused on the topic, but the conclusion can present a wider view of the text.

Essay topics

1 'In *Cloudstreet* tragedy and grief are overcome by hope and forgiveness.' Discuss.

2 '*Cloudstreet* is very Australian but has universal significance.' Discuss.

3 'In *Cloudstreet* Winton demonstrates that there is no single religious path to enlightenment, but many possibilities for achieving this goal.' Discuss.

4 'The two families of *Cloudstreet* live out a microcosmic version of the potential for harmony in the wider world.' Discuss.

5 '*Cloudstreet* is an allegory or morality tale. It is not meant to be read literally.' Discuss.

6 'In *Cloudstreet* all the ends are tied up too neatly to be realistic.' Discuss.

7 'The significance of a dimension beyond the everyday, temporal one is a central tenet of *Cloudstreet*.' Discuss.

8 '*Cloudstreet* demonstrates the potential for breaking patterns of destruction.' Discuss.

9 '*Cloudstreet* illustrates the role of culture in making people feel psychologically and emotionally at home.' Discuss.

10 '*Cloudstreet* can only be properly understood by Australian readers.' Discuss.

Vocabulary for writing on *Cloudstreet*

Acuity: sharpness of thought, understanding, vision or hearing; for example, Fish's heightened understanding.

Apathy: not caring about anything; Dolly is apathetic.

Catharsis: a huge upheaval, relieving a person of a burden, such as when Dolly opens up to Rose about her past.

Dramatic irony: when the reader understands something the characters do not.

Epiphany: a turning point, point of enlightenment.

Ethereal: seemingly not of this world.

Eurhythmy: harmonious proportions; symmetry, rhythmical physical movements. The way a psychological state is shown in the physical and spiritual environment and the three harmonise; for example, the birth of Wax Harry demonstrates eurhythmy through its integration of the physical, spiritual and emotional.

Existentialism: a philosophy or world view that regards it as necessary for people to create their own meaning and live authentically through positive action.

Humanising habitas: the house-as-body, as a character in itself.

Integration: combining of people, things, features or ideas harmoniously.

Internal focalisation: technique whereby the reader has access to the characters' innermost thoughts.

Messianic: saviour-like, as Fish is for his family.

Metaphysical: the spiritual, non-temporal dimension.

Microcosm: a little world within the world, a miniature; the house and two families are a microcosm of the potential for connectedness in the world generally.

Motif: a repeated image, recurring theme or idea; in *Cloudstreet*, 'home' is a motif.

Numinous: mysterious, suggestive of a supernatural presence; for example, the talking pig.

Omnipotent: all-powerful, as are God and Sam's 'Hairy Hand' or 'Shifty Shadow'.

Omnipresent: always there, like water and the river.

Omniscient: all-knowing; the Aboriginal 'prophet' is an example.

Pentecostal: relating to the mystical workings of the Holy Spirit, for example, the talking pig.

Redemption: being saved.

Scatology: vulgar language, 'toilet humour', usually employed for realism.

Subjectivity: one's personal response to and understanding of the world around them.

Symbol: an image representing a profound truth or idea.

Sympathetic/antipathetic characters: those we like, care about, and those that we don't.

Tenets: the foundations of a belief system; the Ten Commandments are tenets of Christianity.

Transcendent: beyond the range of mere human and physical experience; existing apart from the limits of the material world. To transcend: to rise above one's circumstances or feelings of despair, as Dolly does following her unburdening to Rose.

Verisimilitude: 'truth-likeness'; can be achieved through realistic descriptions of people and places; also through the use of actual facts (e.g. the 'Nedlands Monster') that make a story more realistic.

Analysing a sample topic

'*Cloudstreet* can only be properly understood by Australian readers.' Discuss.

Sample introduction

> Tim Winton's epic novel *Cloudstreet* is quintessentially Australian, as evidenced in its vernacular, settings and general world view. As such, Australian readers can relate to it with relative ease, although some of the more historical vocabulary is unfamiliar to modern Australians. The significance of the novel lies in its central tenets which are relevant to almost all humans, regardless of time and place. These include humanity's relationship with God – however that concept is perceived – and the importance of community, family and belonging. As a result of such universality, the novel has been translated into numerous languages and enjoys bestseller status almost 20 years after publication.

Body paragraph outline

Paragraph 1: explain how the novel uses various strategies to appeal to a broad audience beyond one which is defined by nationality.

- The growing interest in spiritualism and revival of churches, and the move towards interfaith movements, underpins the need for a spiritual dimension and for acceptance of differences.
- This is demonstrated in *Cloudstreet* with the comfortable integration of, and narrative sympathy for, Aboriginal prophesy with traditional Christian beliefs and pagan superstition.
- A very human capacity for doubt and loss of faith exists when tragedy and suffering intervene.

Paragraph 2: discuss the importance of learning from history and not allowing its destructive elements to define subsequent generations.

- This is manifest in *Cloudstreet* where forgiveness (such as that between Dolly and Rose or between Dolly and Oriel) brings about renewal (the birth of Harry; the uniting of two long-estranged families).
- This relationship between forgiveness and renewal echoes international experiences – for example, in many nations where atrocities have occurred and where forgiveness creates the conditions for new beginnings.

Paragraph 3: discuss the need for connection in the novel; this is a universal human need, appealing not just to Australian readers.

- People all over the world strive for a homeland – this indicates the need to belong. The *Cloudstreet* characters' needs to reconnect with home and family, despite those families being flawed, is pivotal to their psychological and spiritual wellbeing (Quick's escape from home and family provides an example of what happens when these connections are thwarted).
- Psychological problems and antisocial behaviour result when people are alienated. This is manifest in all the characters who refuse to acknowledge it. Even the serial killer in the novel wants a connection with his son in death.

Sample conclusion

Cloudstreet is set in the most isolated capital in the world, an Australian city teetering on the edge of the Indian Ocean. Certainly the alienation felt profoundly by Winton's characters is exacerbated by the vastness of Australian landscapes and seascapes. However, alienation of the soul can and does happen in any temporal or spatial setting. The values upheld and celebrated by the narrative, such as loyalty, family, acceptance, love, forgiveness and community, are universal and – as is suggested by the synthesis of two absolutely disparate families – could ameliorate many of the world's problems if embraced. Number One Cloud Street houses two families who come to terms with their personal agonies and lack of acceptance and learn to finally live together in harmony. As such, *Cloudstreet* shows, in microcosm, what is possible on a larger scale, and this can be appreciated on many levels by readers of other nationalities.

SAMPLE ANSWER

'The significance of a dimension beyond the everyday, temporal one is a central tenet of *Cloudstreet*.' Discuss.

In Tim Winton's *Cloudstreet*, the inhabitants of the great rambling house which provides the physical setting for most of the novel are, to an extent, affected profoundly by their spiritual lives even if it is simply to vehemently to deny such an effect. Even the 'house-as-body' seems to have an emotional and spiritual life, as it responds to the pain of its inhabitants. The personified house carries biblical associations too, since the narrative's driving necessity is for the house to be set in order, redolent of the Old Testament notion of setting God's house or world in order. The inhabitants of Cloudstreet exhibit much of the unease associated with the human search for a spiritual dimension alongside the struggle to be authentic according to a personal moral framework. The novel's central motif of homecoming is a metaphor for returning to a spiritual homeland, something the characters scorn, reject or simply ignore until they eventually recognise that something vital is missing from their lives. This is precisely why the characters always need to return to Cloudstreet.

Oriel Lamb strays only as far as the backyard, setting herself up in a tent where she sleeps each night. This retreat to the tent can be read as a symbolic return to the womb for Oriel, having experienced little mother-love herself and having been a carer all her life. She rejects the everyday existence of the house itself, of being surrounded by family, of being a real wife to Lester. In the tent, Oriel can escape the exigencies of family life at night and simply exist: 'I wish I could lace it up an never come out ... You could slip food under the flap and I'd never see a soul'. But she knows something is missing and that her self-alienation is not sustainable. Even after telling Lester in no uncertain terms that she has rejected God, the family is aware that she still reads the Bible out in the tent, almost sulkily, suggesting that she aches for something spiritual which is absent or missing. The eventual folding up of the tent and returning inside is a spiritual 'rebirth'. Her hostility towards God is something she has in common with Sam Pickles, although she is be unable to see or acknowledge this.

There is an intensely personal and heartfelt connection between Sam and his creator. Sam's faith is epitomised in an ongoing bond. The 'Hairy Hand' is Sam's nickname for 'Lady Luck', that entity which usually lets him down. By contrast, the nickname Sam accords God – the 'Shifty Shadow' – appears somewhat intimate in tone, yet still spectral, ethereal, suggesting the supernatural nature of God. This again endorses the concept of a relational yet omnipotent being, simultaneously animate and inanimate. This God is an entity whose conduct he does not understand, yet in whom he believes unwaveringly and respects in the manner of the biblical requirement for humans to fear God: 'Well the shadow was on him, the Hairy Hand of God, and he knew that being a man was the saddest, most useless thing that could happen to someone'.

When eurhythmy, or a synthesis, of his temporal life and his relationship with God occurs towards the novel's end, Sam is shown to be relieved and happier, with hope for the future. Sam's long-running conviction that all is random is a possibility that Lester Lamb toys with for a time, but which he can never quite entertain.

Lester Lamb habitually plays a light-hearted game of chance with his family, using a spinning knife to delegate household chores. At one point in his soul-sickness, he wonders if the knife which 'never lies' represents an entirely arbitrary universe, devoid of meaning or any guiding hand. Lester, though, has never completely given up on God, although he claims to have at certain points, such as when he says 'no one believes anymore: the disappointment has been too much'. The Anzac Club does not provide the God-substitute he hoped it would, so he is constantly left with the sense of a void. He confesses his confusion to Oriel, hoping for some reassurance, and her angry cynicism shocks him. She replies, 'Lester, I believe in eight hours' sleep and a big breakfast'. Lester gives himself up to a kind of world-weariness and, as a result, misses many of the signs placed in front of him, such as the Aboriginal man and Fish's visionary observations in the bath and with the pig. While he is saddened by the loss of his religious conviction, Lester is too preoccupied to notice the manifestations of grace, which the reader can see clearly. His relief when the integration of all the elements of his life helps him to see them is palpable. Of course, it is Fish who opens this potentiality.

Fish Lamb is a 'fish' out of water, living in the world but not of the world, in essence more eternal than temporal. He finally becomes fully integrated when he drowns a second time. Fish is a visionary of a kind, exhibiting that which Winton calls a 'positive naiveté', having drowned in his temporal life. By way of his numinous experiences on a level not accessible to those, like Oriel, who are too preoccupied and embittered to see, readers can connect with the overarching principle that acceptance of the gift of grace means 'we all join up somewhere in the end'.

The principal characters of *Cloudstreet* eventually, sometimes even grudgingly, come to accept their place in a spirit-filled landscape, acknowledging that a greater power emanates from somewhere beyond themselves. They begin to understand that their acceptance and personalisation of these gifts will render grace active in their lives and take them home.

REFERENCES & READING

Text

Winton, Tim 1998, *Cloudstreet*, Penguin, Camberwell.

Other references

Batchelor, Elise 1994, *Eurhythmics in the Novels and Short Stories of Tim Winton*, MA Thesis, Monash University.

Ben-Messahel, Sahlia 2006, *Mind the Country: Tim Winton's Fiction*, University of Western Australia Press, Crawley.

Bennett, Bruce 1991, 'The Hills are Alive', in *An Australian Compass: Essays on Place and Direction in Australian Literature*, Fremantle Arts Centre Press, Fremantle, pp.97–112.

Goonan, Michael 1996, *A Community of Exiles: Exploring Australian Spirituality*, St Paul's Publications, Sydney.

Kohn, Rachael, 2005, 'Tim Winton's Faith: Interview with Tim Winton', in *Zadok Perspectives* vol. 86, pp.12–15.

McGirr, Michael 1997, 'Go Home Said the Fish', in *Meanjin*, vol. 56 no. 1, pp.56–66.

——1999, *Tim Winton: The Writer and his Work*, Macmillan Education Australia, Melbourne.

McPhee, Hilary (ed.) 1999, *Tim Winton: A Celebration*, National Library of Australia, Canberra.

Rossiter, Richard and Jacobs, Lyn (eds) 1993, *Reading Tim Winton*, Angus and Robertson, Sydney.

Salter, Owen 1987, 'Suspicious of Hope in a Chaotic World', in *On Being*, June, pp.7–10.

Taylor, Andrew 1996, 'Littoral Erosion: The Changing Shoreline of Australian Culture', in *Australian Literary Studies*, vol. 17 no. 3, pp.248–89.

Thomas, Roie 2008, 'Existentialism in the Fiction of Tim Winton', MA thesis, University of Tasmania.

Vittorin-Vangerud, Nancy 2002, 'Sea-ing Faith, Fathoming Faith', in *Eremos*, vol. 79.

Watzke, Beth 1992, 'Writing the West: Regionalism and Western Australia', in *Westerly*, vol. 37 no. 1, pp.21–9.

Willbanks, Ray 1991, *Speaking Volumes: Australian Writers and Their Work*, Penguin, Ringwood.